To

M000036373

Bobby Brown
and Richie Blue

A Spiritual Memoir

Richard Penaskovic
and
Robert Penaskovic

novitiate, you took the discipline
seriously. I heard loud sounds
from your room as you beat
the bed assiduosly instead of
your back.   Rich Penaskovic

Hamilton Books
A member of
The Rowman & Littlefield Publishing Group
Lanham • Boulder • New York • Toronto • Plymouth, UK

Copyright © 2010 by
Hamilton Books
4501 Forbes Boulevard
Suite 200
Lanham, Maryland 20706
Hamilton Books Acquisitions Department (301) 459-3366

Estover Road
Plymouth PL6 7PY
United Kingdom

Library of Congress Control Number: 2009934913
ISBN: 978-0-7618-4909-4 (paperback : alk. paper)
eISBN: 978-0-7618-4910-0

Cover photo: The Penaskovic twins.

For our children, Kristin Penaskovic, Mary Beth Ruthen, Mark Penaskovic, Kenan Penaskovic, and Nadine Penaskovic, our grandchildren, Leah Sarah Ruthen, Abby Rachel Ruthen, Kaia Pea Topping, Michael John Penaskovic, Anna Marie Penaskovic, and future generations of their children. We sincerely hope that we have been able to give our children both roots and wings. We feel that raising one's children is the most important thing one does in life.

Contents

Preface

In a way telling stories resembles breathing. We do it spontaneously, without conscious effort. We need not focus on breathing directly, except, that is, when we have difficulty catching our breath, such as when climbing a mountain or when we develop asthma. Like breathing, storytelling, too, can be imperceptible. Why so? It's so interwoven into the fabric of our lives that we do not attend to it.

However, storytelling can be imperceptible for another reason. Since the Scientific Revolution storytelling has taken a backseat to science, when the world was reduced to its empirical, phenomenal reality, and mathematics replaced theology as the queen of the sciences. Compared to astrophysics, rocket science, and nanotechnology, telling stories does not seem to count very much today in our high-tech, computer-savvy world.

Stories have the uncanny ability to make us laugh and, correspondingly, to make us cry. In writing this spiritual memoir we have noticed that stories also make us whole. They gather together the separate parts of ourselves and manage to piece them together in a meaningful way. Writing this memoir, then, has been an exercise in self-discovery. We have learned many new things about ourselves just by writing. It seems that in the writing the good things have come.

This book chronicles the spiritual journey of a set of twins, Bobby and Richie Penaskovic from Bayonne, New Jersey. They had to deal with the breakup of their family when they were six years old and lived in three different families by the time they were nine. They depended on each other for emotional survival and learned to trust in God at an early age when their family had to deal with a crisis.

Both boys were close emotionally and seemed to have mental telepathy. They eventually became Franciscan priests with Bobby pursuing his studies in the United States while Richie studying in Wuerzburg and Munich.

These were the heady days of the Sixties and the Second Vatican Council (1962–1965). Both men were affected by the whirlwind of changes inaugurated by the Council. Just as both felt called to the priestly ministry, so too, both felt called by God to leave the active priesthood. Both married nursing supervisors who were former nuns. Bobby found his new vocation doing psychotherapy while Richie found his niche by becoming a college professor at Auburn, a major research university in Alabama.

This book casts a wide beam of light on urban life in New Jersey in the Fifties, the psyche of twins, and the changes in the Catholic Church in the pre-and post-Vatican II eras. It documents how the most difficult spiritual odyssey goes inward where it touches raw nerve.

Acknowledgments

We wish to thank all those who have read and commented on this book in draft form. A semester at the Institute for Ecumenical and Cultural Affairs at St. John's in Collegeville, Minnesota in 2001 gave Richie the opportunity to begin work on this book. Several relatives and friends were particularly helpful in reading the manuscript and offering suggestions. Nancy Penaskovic, Vincent Bolger, Doris Suarez, Russell Siller, Sr. Sean Peters, C.S.J., Jay Lamar, Bill Buskist, Catherine Perricone, David Martin, Patrick Henry, Burt Katz, Mary Belk, our late aunt, Mary Albanese, and scores of others, read an earlier draft of this book for which we are most grateful. Bob's wife, Theresa Penaskovic, deserves a special word of thanks for suggesting the title for this book. Auburn University, in the person of the Provost, John Heilman, deserves a special word of thanks. Dr. Heilman gave Richie a sabbatical during the 2008–2009 academic years during which time Rich worked with Bob to complete this memoir. Justin Dealy did yeoman work in preparing this manuscript for publication. We have become aware that we did not create ourselves. Rather, we owe our identity to the various communities that have formed us, our family, the Conventual Franciscan friars, the community at the College of Saint Rose, and the Auburn University community. To all we say "Thanks."

Chapter One

City Kids

"All sorrows can be borne if you put them in a story."

Isak Dineson

"It is in your power to review your life, to look at things you saw before, from another point of view."

Soren Kierkegaard

This memoir concerns the story of two identical twins: Bobby Brown and Richie Blue. Bobby wore brown clothes while Richie wore blue so folks could tell us apart. We did so to accommodate others. Inside, we loved it when folks confused us. This proved to be fun, one peculiar way for us to get a leg up on the world. The bond we forged with one another might best be described as primitive, biological, coming from one egg, transcending space and time.

As small children and even today, one of us can sometimes start a sentence and the other finish it, often using the same identical words. Or we might blurt out the same line at the same exact time, almost on cue. This often takes even us by surprise. We once told Mom what a pretty dress she wore, coming out with the same comment simultaneously. In school we felt we could use mental telepathy to give answers to questions which our twin did not know. How did this happen? We weren't quite sure. Was it genetic or environmental? Did it come from sharing the womb with our twin and every waking moment thereafter with a mirror image of another? Might this count as some kind of extraordinary knowing?

In the Forties life resembled a golden bracelet of charms. Computers were the stuff of science fiction and the T.V. had not yet been in vogue. The world

1

appeared to be rather simple and folks generally felt very secure. For all practical purposes crime did not exist and a young child could feel safe walking the streets of Bayonne, New Jersey. Our lives revolved around our families, Frank Penaskovic, our dad, Jean del Soldato, mom, our older brother, Frank, Bobbie and Richie, the twins, Bill, and baby brother, Tommy.

We twins were "cradle Catholics," born into a very devout and religious family. We said grace before meals, attended church on Sunday, and would never go to bed without reciting night prayers on our knees. After all, Mom and Dad modeled this behavior for us and taught us to pray. In the Penaskovic family prayer seemed as natural as breathing and just as vital.

We loved being together as kids, looking into each other's face and seeing a mirror image of our own. How comforting to know we had a place of refuge against the world's harsh winds, our arms locked together as we sauntered down 43rd Street in Bayonne, New Jersey, the neighbors inside their homes observing us through their front windows, recognizing us together, Bobby Brown and Richie Blue, one for all and all for one.

We were protective of each other. Once when another boy gave one of us a hard time, the other jumped him from behind and brought him to the ground. We were in tune with each other's feelings, and we learned the importance of reading other people carefully. We lived in several different families growing and knew experientially how to pick up vibes from those around us, in order to fit in with others and our surroundings.

We grew up on 43rd Street, between Avenue A and Avenue C in Bayonne in a mostly white, neighborhood except for the many black families that lived around the corner on 44th Street. As kids we attended St, Vincent's Catholic Church where most of the parishioners were either Irish or Italian.

Seven blocks away lived mom's family, staunchly Italian. Our maternal grandmother, Elvira, only spoke Italian. Mom had to translate for us what she said. Elvira, a woman of few words, sometimes talked to herself but that did not bother us, although we did find it peculiar. We knew Grandma had her own set of problems. She showed very little affect. She wore the same black dress every time we visited. Dad told us that when her husband bought her a new dress, she threw it into the kitchen stove. We did not ask why. We only visited them sporadically. On one visit Dad sat down in one of the kitchen chairs and it collapsed in front of us. Dad had this startled look on his face and we dared not laugh. Later, when back at home, our family, in unison, gave out a hearty belly-laugh over this incident.

Mom's stepfather, Vincent, liked to drink wine which he made in the cellar. Dad told us that they had wine coming out of the faucet instead of water. Grandpa Scapigliati had Dad over once to help him paint the house. Before beginning, Grandpa toasted Dad with a glass of homemade red wine. Then,

Grandpa gave Dad another glass of wine for the paintbrush, followed by one for the first stroke of the brush. By the time Dad began to paint he was half-looped and almost fell off the ladder.

Grandma lived in a predominately Italian neighborhood, complete with Italian grocery stores, and a Catholic church where the priests spoke Italian. Her first husband, Louis Del Soldato, had died in the old country when Mom was just a toddler. Her second husband, Vincent Scapigliati, a stonemason, did not look kindly on religion. He thought that the church simply wanted to make money and refused to attend.

Mom lived in the Scapigliati home. Elvira and Vince had two children of their own, Marie and John who everyone called "Teddy." Her step-dad tended to be stricter with her and more easy-going with her step-sister, Marie, and her step-brother, Teddy. She never felt she could please her step-dad. Mom had some girl friends but very few close friends. When problems developed later on when she had five young children, she had no one to turn to for advice.

Marie married Vince Albanese and lived upstairs on 19 A East 51st Street. They had three children, Marilyn, Vinnie, Jr. and Angela. Marilyn developed serious mental problems as a teenager and has spent fifty years in a mental institution. Aunt Marie and Uncle Vince would sometimes take us sleigh riding down Hudson County Park, snow permitting, or pile us into their station wagon and take us to a drive-in movie. That sticks out in our memory as a real treat.

BAYONNE: COSMOPOLITAN CITY

Johnny Carson on the *Tonite Show* regularly got a round of laughs when he referred to a fictional character, Raoul from Bayonne. The city derived its name from one of its streets, Bayonne Avenue. We think of Bayonne as the city of ethnic diversity and one of the best cities in the entire State of New Jersey. Bayonne has proximity to the Big Apple with its bright lights and Broadway shows. The oil refinery founded there and run by the Standard Oil Company since at least 1877 gave the city a distinctive odor, although that's not the case today.

In the late 1860s residents of New York City, including authors and artists flocked to Bayonne to enjoy its resort hotels and clean beaches on both Newark Bay and New York Bay. Henry Meigs, Jr., president of the New York Stock Exchange, served as the first mayor. Bayonne supplied fish and oysters to Manhattan residents. It became an industrialized city in the late nineteenth and early twentieth century, a place many European immigrants called home, including our grandparents on our father's side, John Penaskovic and Anna Bodnar, and John Scapigliati and Elvira del Soldato on our mother's side.

During World War II Bayonne became home to a large shipping terminal, the Military Ocean Terminal, built on man-made land jutting out from the east side of Bayonne into New York Bay. It boasted the largest dry-docks on the Eastern seaboard and the location of a vast naval center. When we Penaskovic twins were small we used to visit this huge naval base on Memorial Day and take a tour of battleships and aircraft carriers, which tickled us with their sheer size.

A place may be understood as a portion of space vested with particular significance. One may think of place, then, as "interpreted space." A place, such as our native city, Bayonne, forms a complex network of connections, continuities, and relationships of cultural, physical, and social conditions that describe our actions, awareness, and responses. Bayonne gave both content and shape to our lives as twins. We see Bayonne as the point of origin for our spiritual journey. It's the place and setting where we have wrestled our story out of the circumstances of family and location.

THE FASCINATION OF WATER

The kids in our gang called us the Twins. We learned to be who we are by relating to the landscapes of our childhood in Bayonne. We grew up with a fascination for water because Bayonne is a peninsula, surrounded by New York Bay, Newark Bay, and the Kill van Kull. It seems to us that the power of place derives more from personal and collective associations or from cultural factors than it does from something inherent to the place itself. We both love to fish. When we lived with the Bolgers, our cousins, Paulie and Vinnie, took us crabbing down 49th Street. Paulie or Vinnie would put one of us on the handlebars of his bike and pedal about three miles to New York Bay. We would hold the six-foot long "scap" net, the killie net, bread, and a penknife. It always proved to be a real adventure because the bicyclist had to dart his way in and out of traffic on Avenue E, which had a lot of eighteen-wheeler trucks.

Down at New York Bay a varied assortment of barges sunken in mud made a great place for crabbing. These barges provided a convenient framework for our first swim lessons. One had to do the breaststroke to avoid the garbage in the water.

We were particularly delighted to "scap up" a blue crab or soft shell crab, which were simply mouth-watering to eat. Crabs were a cinch to cook. They had to be put in a pot of boiling water with salt, pepper, and a little lemon thrown in for good measure. New York Bay proved to be a good place to catch eels, which we did as teenagers, renting a boat at 30th Street and rowing out to a good spot. Eel amazed us because they continued to move in the frying pan after they were killed. Our cousin, Paulie, bought a small cabin cruiser and would take us fishing off Sandy Hook and Belmar, New Jersey.

We learned at an early age to have great respect for the ocean. One day while fishing off Coney Island, we got caught in a thunderstorm that came up suddenly in the heat of summer. As if the huge waves and lightning were not enough to strike terror in the hearts of two-ten-year olds, the engine on our boat died. We faced the prospect of being hurled onto the rocky shore by the wind and waves. Luckily, Paulie, a good mechanic, got the engine started just as we were about 75 feet off shore. God heard our prayer that day.

ETHNIC RIVALS

As children we remember the various ethnic groups that lived in enclaves scattered throughout the city: the Irish, the Slovaks, the Polish, the Italians, the Russians, and the Jews. In the Thirties and Forties young folks had enormous pressure put on them to marry someone from their own ethnic background. When Dad, a Slovak, married Mom, an Italian, both families were upset. Tensions continued particularly when at the birth of our older brother, Frank, in 1939 Grandpa Scapigliati served pigeon to the assembled guests. The Slovaks were indignant that they were invited to eat pigeon at a baptismal repast. This was definitely not part of their culture.

The Slovaks and the Italians were worlds apart culturally and in terms of their ethos. Our Italian grandfather would buy a baby turkey several months before Thanksgiving and let it live and grow in his basement, feeding it to its heart's content. Then, he would slaughter it the day before Thanksgiving when it became nice and plump. At this the Slovaks could only shrug their shoulders.

Dad's parents were from the present-day Slovak Republic and met here in Bayonne at St. Joseph's Church, which catered to Slovak immigrants. People from the Eastern bloc countries had a certain paranoia when they came to this country around 1900. And our grandfather, John Penaskovic, who did not speak English very well, worked for Esso, now known as the Exxon Corporation. Slovak immigrants felt less vulnerable and powerless in working for a large multinational company. Unions were attractive to immigrants because they were a source of appeal if there were conflicts with their employer. Many immigrants could be taken advantage of since they were simple folk, and often illiterate, like our grandfather. Most of our Slovak relatives were inclined to work for a large employer. Perhaps that's what attracted Dad to work for General Motors and to continue working there even when times got rough.

Our mother's family came from the small towns of Onano and Grotto di Castro in the region between Florence and Rome, Italy. They were accustomed to being self-employed entrepreneurs. One of our Italian relatives, a shoemaker, made shoes for Pope Pius XII. Our Aunt Marie and Uncle Vinnie owned an Italian grocery store, as did our Uncle Vinnie's brother.

Our Italian grandfather made his own wine and a brandy or distilled wine that was very potent called "grappa." He did this in the basement of his home. As kids we liked going there to taste a little wine with our meals and watching Grandpa who worked as a mason, crack open a walnut with the strength of one hand. Once when we visited Grandpa he could not climb the stairs to his second floor apartment. He ordered Grandma, Elvira, to get him some of his wine from the basement. After drinking a glass, he waited a few minutes and promptly climbed the stairs with no problem.

Today people from India own many of the stores on Broadway, the main shopping thoroughfare. Correspondingly, Muslims, who speak Arabic, own the gas stations. On a recent visit to Bayonne, Richie spoke Arabic to a Muslim in a gas station on Avenue E. He seemed genuinely surprised that an American could engage him in conversation in his native language. Many native residents of Bayonne see the influx of people from India and the Mideast as a "foreign invasion." On reflection, though, every city remains in constant flux. When our grandparents came from the Slovak Republic at the turn of the century they, too, were looked down upon by the Dutch and other natives of Bayonne.

In the sacred quality of place, such as the City of Bayonne, the deepest meaning of existence, yes, even the sacred, is evoked in our lives. We remember riding our bikes over Bayonne Bridge and surveying the landscape of the city as a whole. This remains in our memory as an intimation of the sacred, a gaze on the holy.

OUR INFANCY

Our story begins with our birth on February 11, 1941. That year such notables as Lou Gehrig, James Joyce, Henri Bergson, R. Tagore, and Virginia Woolf died. February 11th will always be a special day in our family. Richie's wife, Nancy, was born on that exact day and year 160 miles away in Schenectady, New York, and our younger brother, Bill, celebrated his birthday on that same day in 1946. In addition to Mom and Dad, our family consisted of five boys: Frank, the oldest, Bob, Rich, (the Twins), Bill, and Tom.

Dad met Mom in a factory that made garments. Mom had jet-black hair and Dad found her to be very attractive. Dad, a handsome young man, worked as a mechanic in the factory, fixing machines that developed problems. They dated for about a year until Dad asked Mom to marry him. They rented an apartment on West 43rd Street and decided to have a family. When Mom at age 24 became pregnant with us twins, she and Dad had trouble making ends meet. Hence Dad had to sell his prize possession, a 1939 Packard car. That involved a huge sacrifice on Dad's part.

We carry within us all the places we have ever been. However, our first home occupies a special place in our hearts. We can still remember the view from our mother's arms or father's shoulder as they carried us about as infants. Mom usually fed Bobby and Dad took care of Richie. Perhaps that's why in later life Bob felt closer emotionally to Mom and Richie to Dad. It all goes back to the hand that rocked the cradle.

While Bob tended to idealize Mom throughout her life, Richie idealized Dad. At graduation from St. Joseph's elementary school, a professional photographer took a group picture of the graduates with the pastor and eighth-grade teacher. These pictures were then displayed in the hall of St. Joseph's school for all to see. Richie had seen Dad's picture in the hall of the school and in his graduation picture held his face the same way Dad did at his graduation.

How did we experience God? We experienced God in our family. When we were about five years old we remember seeing Dad kneeling down at the side of his bed and saying his prayers. Both Mom and Dad instructed us on how to pray, at least to say formal prayers. It seems that in the home each child comes face to face with the beliefs, meanings, and values of a wider community. Each home has its own "field of rules." And the message we received as little tykes was this: prayer is an essential part of life.

Mom tended to be lenient with us. And patient. She would make a delicious Italian soup called pasta fazool in Italian dialect. Mom, a talented seamstress, made us adorable outfits. She would read the Sunday funnies to us. We grew up reading about the Katz'n Jammer kids and Dick Tracy, who had on his wrist a short wave radio, the size of a watch. This seemed totally incredible to us at the time, but not today when youngsters have I phones, palm pilots, and blackberry phones.

Dad and Mom took us often for a walk to Hudson County Park, which faced Newark Bay. Dad would take pictures of the three boys, Frank and the Twins, and would develop and enlarge the photos himself. Hudson County Park, an oasis of green in a totally urban environment, had a quarter-mile track made of cinders, small pools where we sailed our miniature boats, a pond where one could ice skate, and hills to sled down under the watchful eyes of Mom and Dad. It also boasted a gorgeous view of Newark Bay where one could fish or go crabbing.

Mom let us run in the rain with no shirts on during the start of a thunderstorm on hot, muggy summer days. We built stilts out of wood and enjoyed walking on them. Our older brother, Frankie, had a lot of imagination and we looked up to him, our natural leader. He taught us to jump from the roof of a small shack in the back of our house on West 43rd Street. He said that if we jumped with our umbrella opened, we could magically "fly like Superman." Of course we believed him, though our faith languished when we hit the ground full force.

Mom treated us royally as kids. She would send us to the corner grocery store to buy small items. Bob could always be trusted with money because he was five minutes older than Richie and played the role of an elder brother to the hilt. Richie felt completely comfortable playing second fiddle to his twin. During the war years the government rationed certain items. Each family could only get coupons for a certain amount of sugar each month. At night we sometimes heard the warning sirens telling us to pretend it was a real air attack and to take cover. So we turned out all the lights and took cover under the bed. What great fun. This made our life exciting.

Our early years were not all fun and games. Mom and Dad had huge arguments. Mom would throw things and on several occasions piled several large items of furniture against the door so that Dad could not get in the house when he returned from work. Dad asked one of the priests from St. Joseph's Church to talk to Mom but that did not change things very much. Big trouble lay ahead.

Our family went each Sunday to Mass at St. Vincent's Church located four blocks from our house. We remember walking down the aisle for Mass when we were five years old. We had on our little beanie hats and had forgotten to take them off. Some stranger took off our hats and handed them to us. We were insulted by this man's rudeness.

From an early age our parents dressed us alike. We looked so similar we have trouble deciding who is whom when viewing our early baby pictures. We shared everything. Once Bobby wanted gum that Richie had in his mouth. So, without hesitation, and throwing hygiene to the winds, Richie gave Bobby half of the gum. Like all kids, though, we did have our squabbles. Fifteen minutes after Bobby was taken to the doctors for stitches received from a nail on a stick Richie hit him with, Richie had to be taken to the doctors for stitches because Bobby reciprocated in kind. We both have scars above our moustaches that document this incident.

A TRAUMATIC EVENT

When we were six years old our childhood world, like Humpty Dumpty, came tumbling down. The straw that broke the camel's back happened quickly. One day, Mom had turned on the gas jets in the house and Dad smelled gas when he walked in from work. Dad feared that Mom had intended to light a match to the gas. He decided then and there that Mom had to be confined to a mental hospital. The entire event stands out poignantly in our memories. We were so shocked to see Mom kicking and yelling as she was forcibly taken from us that our feelings were numb, frozen if you will. We were horrified. It seemed like a bad dream. The full meaning of what happened took years for us to process. This had to be an excruciating decision for Dad to make. It would mean the breakup of our family.

Mom received a diagnosis of paranoid schizophrenia. Dad told us this after our first visit to the hospital in terms we could understand. He told us that Mom had a difficult time coping with life. He did not use the word, paranoid schizophrenia, but told us that Mom had an illness and had to be confined to the hospital for a time. In speaking of what happened in terms we could understand, Dad made it easier for us to cope with a terrible situation. We remember this as one of the best things Dad did for us.

Another thing that Dad pulled off is this: he talked his sister, Helen, into taking us twins into their home instead of separating us. That decision proved crucial to our emotional survival. We would have each other to lean on in times of troubled water. In a sense our older brother, Frank, had the toughest adjustment of anyone. He would be inserted into the life of another family with no one to lean on when times got tough.

Our hearts seemed to shut down after Mom was hospitalized in 1947. We were six years old at the time. We will never forget the sadness seeing her on that first day at the county hospital in Secaucus, New Jersey. Mom, dressed in a drab smock, cried upon seeing Dad and her five boys, ranging in age from six months old to eight. We visited her practically every Sunday for the next twenty years. Saying "Goodbye" each time proved to be heart-wrenching for all of us.

Frankie, the oldest, had just a few months ago celebrated his eighth birthday. He would now live with his uncle, Larry, and his wife, aunt Julia. Bill, age two, and Tommy, the youngest, a mere six months old, and Dad moved in with our grandparents Anna and John. The Christmas of 1947 turned out to be a nightmare. Billy came down with scarlet fever and had to be taken by ambulance to the Jersey City Medical Center. Frankie and Richie also had scarlet fever but were able to deal with it, including 104-degree temperatures, because they were older than Bill. Dad had placed a quarantine sign near the entrance of our house on instructions from our family physician, Dr. Aronowitz. Happily for us, physicians still made house calls. At the time we had a blizzard and there were piles of snow on the ground.

In retrospect we see this incident as the culmination of years of violent arguments between Mom and Dad. WWII raged for the first four years of our life. The Allies were pitted against the Axis nations of Japan, Germany, and Italy. This war paled in significance for us compared to the war going on between Dad and Mom. And we were too young to distinguish the good guy from the enemy. We remember seeing Mom throw large items like radios and an ironing board at Dad. Some of these items would go smashing against the walls of the house. Yet Dad had difficulty expressing his anger directly to Mom. He tended to give the silent treatment if he was upset. And this only served to raise Mom's frustration level.

As a result of this experience we twins developed a soft spot in our hearts for the sufferings of the mentally ill and their families, as well as for prisoners and their families. It seems so unfair for children to be cut off from their parents, particularly their children, no matter what the reason. Children have very limited power to verbalize what happens to them. Perhaps that's why young children in India are kept with their mothers in prison. This may seem strange to us but it makes good sense to keep mothers and children together particularly those under the age of seven.

Most of the memories we have about this time revolve around playing outdoors, such as playing in the park, making stilts and jumping from the garage roof. We cannot even remember what our kitchen or bedroom looked like, probably because what happened indoors, the tension between Dad and Mom, evoked memories too painful to remember and were, therefore, squeezed out of consciousness.

A SILVER LINING

Where did God figure into all of this? That Christmas the three older boys, Frank, Bob and Rich, were, thanks to divine providence, given a train set complete with bells and whistles. It even had a bright light on the engine. We would often run this Lionel train at night in a dark house. We did not know it then, but the men at General Motors who worked with Dad chipped in to buy us this train set. We think of it as a little glimmer of joy in a troubled time, an oasis in a time of severe drought. Even though these were difficult times this train set completely captivated us. It served to divert our attention from the loss of our mom, although the pain of separation would gnaw at us for the next decade. Like arthritis, it came at us like a daily dose of pain.

We also had a giant jigsaw puzzle, a present from Dad's first cousin, Johnny Gala, set up on the living room table. This huge puzzle took days to put together correctly. To this day we are less than fond of jigsaw puzzles because too many painful memories are associated with them. Johnny also gave us an Army set that completely enthralled us. There were tanks, trucks, and jeeps made completely out of cardboard.

GENERAL MOTORS

Like his own father, Dad could be hard to please, and could, at times, be demanding of others. Dad's job made great demands on him, physically speaking. He would rise at 4:15 A.M. to get ready. He had to commute to Linden, New Jersey, where he worked on the assembly line for General Motors. The line served as his personal tyrant. Dad could not even go the bathroom unless he first found a substitute who could keep the assembly line rolling.

Dad's foreman at the plant constantly tried to re-assign him to work that fell outside the scope of his job, according to the union contract with management. The "time and motion" studies of Dad's work revealed that he performed the work of two and one-half men. After a while Dad hated General Motors so much so that when we got to be working age, he absolutely refused to let us put in an application, nor did he ask us to attend the Christmas parties the company put on each year for the children of the employees. Dad would come home from work around four o'clock completely spent and would often fall asleep in his chair.

Mom would be confined to the county mental hospital for the better part of twenty years. They kept her on medication to keep her calm but did absolutely no therapy with her, except for electric shock therapy, which caused her to lose some of her memory. Later on it would come out in an investigation that several of the doctors at the hospital had phony credentials and were not real doctors. How strange, but true.

Dad would take us faithfully each Sunday to visit her. We had to take three buses to get to Secaucus, which was out of the way. The trip could take up to two hours, depending on the bus schedule. We felt scared walking into the mental hospital. It had the combined stench of several hundred patients in it. Some of them yelled obscenities at us. We were often frightened, but after a while learned to ignore those who would "lose" it. Tommy, just an infant at the time our family broke up, did not know Mom. As he got older, he would ask himself "Who is this strange woman at this hospital I'm talking to?"

MEMORIES OF GRANDMA'S HOUSE

After the break-up Dad took the youngest children, Bill and Tom, to Grandma's house. Grandma only had four rooms in her house. She and our grandfather, John, lived there along with two unmarried sons, Stevie and Andy. Grandma and Gramps had one bedroom, quite tiny, and another bedroom, modest in size, where Dad, Bill, and Tom slept. A fold-up bed, which had to be wheeled in and out of the living room each night, provided sleeping quarters for Andy and Stevie. Seven adults had to share one bathroom and it took very little to get on one another's nerves in such tight quarters.

Gramps and Grandma were regarded by the common consensus of the family, that is, all children and grandchildren, as saints. They made the ten-minute walk to Mass at 5:30 A.M. each day. They also stayed for the 7, 8 and 8:30 A.M. masses each day, followed by prayers in Slovak recited by about twenty senior citizens. The streets were occasionally icy, particularly after a snowstorm, and Grandpa in particular was unsteady on his feet because of diabetes and dizziness. Occasionally he would fall on the ice, but for him that did not deter him from going to church. He would simply get up and continue. No one really knew his age because a fire destroyed his baptismal records in his hometown church of Kurov near Bratislava in Slovakia many years before we were born. We celebrated Gramps's birthday on New Year's Day.

NOT EXACTLY HOLY WATER

Although we considered Gramps a saintly person, he made his own booze during Prohibition. He set up a still in the bathtub and made whiskey. Grandma feared the contraption would blow up and set the entire house on fire, and she had visions of police discovering the still and hauling Gramps off to jail for breaking the law of the land. Fortunately for Grandma and for us, none of these fears became reality.

When we visited Grandma's house, Gramps did not usually speak to us. He would be busy with his daily prayer schedule and would not interrupt it to speak to us or to anyone for that matter. There were statues of Mary and pictures of the saints, especially The Little Flower, throughout the small house. It was as if God dwelled in Gramps's house as in a tabernacle. The house had no TV, just a Victrola phonograph to play records. We never saw our grandparents use the Victrola, but we boys took turns winding it up to play. One could play 33, 45, and 78 records.

Grandpa tended to be rigid in his ways. It upset him greatly that Richie ate with his left hand. He insisted that Richie learn to eat with the correct hand, the right one, which he eventually did. He demanded that Grandma have his supper on the table precisely at 5 P.M. Otherwise he would bang the table with his knife and fork. Gramps would say a long silent prayer in Slovak before he ate. He also said a prayer after the meal. Gramps did not speak much. It did not bother him to eat the entire meal in silence. Grandma waited on him hand and foot. Feminism was definitely not in the air back then.

Grandma also had her religious side. She read the Bible each night in Slovak. Grandma had a very simple faith. She only went to grammar school and then started working as a housekeeper. Grandpa could not read and write. He used to sign his name with a big "X." Even as kids we thought it strange that we were asked to help him make that "X" with a pen. As good Catholics, our Slovak grandparents did not eat meat on Friday. They also fasted during Lent and abstained from meat on Wednesday and Saturdays of Lent. They said the rosary each day in Slovak. The Mass itself was in Latin, including the hymns. The celebrant had his back to the people most of the time except for the readings and those times in the liturgy when he would turn around to the congregation and say, "Dominus vobiscum" (the Lord be with you) and the congregation responded, "Et cum spiritu tuo" (and also with you).

St. Joseph's Church served as the focal point of our grandparents' lives. It provided life insurance through the Slovak Catholic Sokol, fraternal societies such as the Knights of Columbus and the Holy Name Society, and the Rosary Altar Society. The church sponsored parish dances where young men and women could meet, the Sodality of the Miraculous Medal for young women, a parish bowling league, the Catholic Youth Organization, a chapter of the Boy Scouts and Girl Scouts, and a parish grammar school.

The priests were highly regarded since they spoke Slovak and English and were well-educated compared to the laity at the time. Rules of living the faith were promulgated from the pulpit and the local bishop gave a very strict interpretation of the rules which were followed religiously by the faithful. The church had regulations on fasting the night before receiving communion, how often to go to confession, fasting and abstinence during Lent, and the correct distance to keep from one's partner while dancing.

OTHER DRIVERS BEWARE

Gramps learned to drive when he turned sixty years old. Dad taught him, in spite of the fact that Gramps only understood Slovak and Dad did not always know the Slovak words for the technical parts of the car. Grandpa drove an old Model T Ford, one that had to be cranked up by hand. Gramps had numerous accidents, which he always paid off in cash since he had no insurance.

The family had an inkling that something was wrong with his sight when he smacked into the back of a bus. The final straw occurred when twice he crashed his car into a fence on a curve on the old Hook Road in Bayonne. Doctors discovered he was blind in one eye and had cataracts in the other. Before any of Gramps' accidents, Grandma resolutely refused to ride in a car with Gramps as the driver. Grandma in her wisdom knew better. And that's why she lived to be 95.

Grandma loved her garden and took great pride in it. She raised roses and peppermint. One day she found a large five-foot snake in the garden and we all wondered how it ever got there since Bayonne is in an urban area. It probably escaped from some ship down at the dock about two miles away and made it to Grandma's backyard. Grandma loved to tell stories, especially about life in the old country. Perhaps she inspired us to write our story.

Gramps died in 1969 and Richie said the funeral Mass. We remember well how we could feel Gramps' presence at his funeral Mass in St. Joseph's church on Avenue E and 25th Street. The family did not go to pieces at his wake and funeral. Our faith supported us. Grandma, in particular, knew that Gramps was "with God" and found this to be a soothing thought. They buried Gramps at Holy Family Cemetery in Jersey City. He had bought a plot there many years before, one with enough room for eight. Today it's not safe to visit this cemetery. Hoodlums often prey on folks who return to visit the grave sites of their loved ones and are robbed at gun or knife-point.

As mentioned above, Grandma lived to be 95. About three weeks before her death, her heart suddenly stopped while she was in Bayonne Hospital. The medical personnel called a Code Blue and revived her, although her heart muscle had worn out completely. Grandma would not have wanted extraordinary measures taken to keep her alive. We noticed more sadness at Grandma's funeral than at Gramps. The family mourned Grandma, the very heart and soul, for many years afterwards. Her death signaled the end of an era.

When we were young, our family, the Lipinski family, and the Lawrence family got together every Christmas and every New Years Day. Grandma would make wonderful bread stuffed with cheese, jelly or nuts. She would spend days cooking and preparing for Christmas. All the kids, that is, all eleven of us would get money from our uncles. This coming together served to cement our families into one. With Grandma's demise this ended.

Easter served a similar function. Grandma would take a basket of Slovak cheese, homemade breads, and ham on Easter Saturday morning to St. Joseph's Church. There the priest would bless the food to be consumed on Easter Sunday. We remember these times at Grandma's house as special. Grandma's house has been torn down and a new one built at 76 East 28th street. When we now ride down that street, a gaggle of happy memories flood our consciousness. We remember and cherish the times that were.

COUNTING OUR BLESSINGS

1. We learned to have an upbeat, optimistic view of life. We tried not to dwell on unpleasant experiences from our past. Instead, we forced ourselves to concentrate on the present.
2. We have always believed in Divine Providence, namely, the doctrine that God speaks to us through the events and happenings of daily life. Those who have a strong belief in a Higher Power always expect things to turn out for the best. A power greater than we injected hope into our veins, a hope that sustained us through thick and thin.
3. From an early age we learned to identify with the underdog and with those who are troubled, needy, and unable to help themselves. Perhaps this accounts for the fact that we felt called to the helping professions, psychotherapy for Bob and teaching for Richie.

Chapter Two

Thank You Lord for Caring Relatives

"Kindness is a language which the deaf can hear and the blind can read."

Mark Twain

"Help your brother's boat across, and your own will reach the shore."

Hindu Proverb

THE LIPINSKI FAMILY

After our family's diaspora in 1948, Frank went to live with the Lawrences, who had four children of their own. We twins were taken in by Dad's sister, Aunt Helen, her husband, Eddie, and their two children, Eleanor and Ed, Jr. Their home had three rooms downstairs and two bedrooms upstairs. Located in the section of Bayonne known as Prospect Avenue many immigrants from Eastern European countries settled in this part of town, in part because housing costs were modest, in part because of its location on the other side of the tracks, separated from Bayonne proper by the railroad.

Life could be tough on the other side of the tracks. If barking dogs were your thing, you would have loved walking along Prospect Avenue. Many of the kids were punks and threw rocks picked up on the unpaved school grounds. This part of town reminded us of the movie with Marlon Brando "On the Waterfront." Some of the older kids sporting black leather jackets, joined gangs, and were ready to mix it up at the drop of a hat. Even the elementary school kids gambled. Almost everyone played the numbers, thanks to the generosity of the candy store owners in the area, who made extra money from bets played by folks on a daily basis. It also brought more customers into the store who bought other items.

Once we developed mumps, accompanied by high fever. Dad visited us to demonstrate his care and concern. He put his hand on Richie's forehead and Richie felt that hand on him for months. Richie thought of it as a sacramental touch of compassion, assurance, and consolation, a divine touch in human form.

We stayed with the Lipinski family for about two years. They were good, God-fearing folk, and we were extremely grateful they took us in when we had no place to go. We loved playing with Eleanor and Ed, Jr. and we would often get silly together at the dinner table, sometimes to the consternation of Uncle Eddie. Uncle Eddie would occasionally take us for a ride in his truck from General Cable Corporation. We would ride down the Hook, (the section of town near the New York Bay), on bumpy roads that would bounce us in the truck so high our heads would almost hit the top. How exhilarating. The Lipinski's had a small dog, named Lucky, who stole our hearts. Lucky liked to chew on things and we were only too happy to let him chew on our corduroy pants. And he obliged willingly, much to the dismay of Aunt Helen, who would have to mend our pants. Perhaps that's why Lucky disappeared one day never to be found.

Uncle Ed helped us with our homework on the kitchen table. He loved to do math, his favorite subject and our worst. In class we sometimes had trouble paying attention. In third grade one of us imagined that the communists invaded our country. We defended our classmates by taking out our machine gun and killing all those who would dare come close. In the Fifties the communist party in the U.S. supposedly had its tentacles everywhere and at school we practiced for a nuclear attack from the Soviet Union. The nun in charge told us to take cover under our desks and to close our eyes so as not to be blinded by the light emitted from an atomic bomb blast. Another nun had a more realistic take on the situation. She told her class not to bother hiding under the desk because it would do no good against a nuclear attack. Instead, the children were instructed to reverently say an "Act of Contrition," in which they begged God to forgive them their sins.

Sunday afternoons seemed to drag on forever. This was not a reflection on the Lipinskis. There were not many kids our age on our street at the time. One classmate, Paul Kulhar, came from a troubled family and we were reluctant to play with him. The boredom of Sunday afternoon changed when the first Christmas there Frank, Bobby and Richie were given a small red Ross bike with training wheels. The three of us had to share the bike and we had no problem doing so. We never had one argument about who would ride the bike next. Frankie had developed rheumatic fever when he was about nine years old and under doctors' orders could not walk or run. He had to be shuffled around in a baby stroller by the Lawrences. That took its toll on him and on the Lawrences as well.

A TRADITION OF SERVICE

Serving as altar boys kept open our connection to God. Dad had been an altar boy as a youth and we continued the family tradition. We had to memorize in Latin the Confiteor and other parts of the Mass and recite them to Sr. Pauline in order to be certified as altar servers. At times we would have to rise at 5 A.M and rush off to serve Msgr. Chmely at the 5:30 A.M. Mass. Aunt Helen had to get up at an early hour and this must have been bothersome to her also.

Father Chmely, the pastor, could be rough on altar boys. He hated it if one even accidentally touched the chalice when pouring wine or water into it. If one poured in too much water he would suddenly take the chalice away so one wound up pouring the water on the floor. He had a huge German shepherd that bared its teeth if you came too close. We surmise he had it for protection in case someone dared steal the collection money in the rectory. The dog did a magnificent job of intimidating small children.

We loved going to funerals. We knew even at a tender age that death played a huge part of life on planet Earth. We would often be given a $1 tip for serving at a funeral Mass. That certainly made our day. We also got to ride in a chauffeured, jet-black, stretch limousine to Holy Cross Cemetery in North Arlington cemetery. That made us feel like big shots.

We once saw a woman try to jump into her husband's casket as it was being lowered into the ground. She had to be restrained. After that incident gravediggers lowered the casket into the ground after the family had left. We were taken with the beauty of songs, such as the *Dies Irae*, that were sung at a funeral Mass and at the cemetery, particularly the song in Latin which asked the angels to lead the soul of the departed into Paradise. We did not find them morbid, but rather uplifting. We particularly liked the smell of incense at the funeral Mass. The smell gave us a slight spiritual high. We imagined heaven peopled by angels all swinging incense, wafting up to the throne of the Almighty.

Father Chmely gave the impression of being cold and aloof. Actually, he had a good heart and could be charming to those who knew him well. He liked to discuss Shakespeare with us when we were in high school. However, most altar boys were afraid of him. We twins avoided going to him for confession for fear he might chew us out for some small infraction. In retrospect, he functioned as a typical pastor in the pre-Vatican II church. The clergy enjoyed such veneration prior to Vatican II that we wondered if the rectory really had a bathroom.

Uncle Ed gave us a bath every Saturday night. He also supervised us shining shoes while we listened to the Phantom on the radio. We went to bed promptly at 8 o'clock just as Gangbusters came on the radio. Uncle Eddie had a temper and many times we were frightened by it. Looking back we realize that underneath his temper he was frightened by all the work Aunt Helen did on our behalf.

What did it feel like living at the Lipinskis? We were basically happy, well cared for, and treated very well, thank you. At times we felt on guard, that is, there were so many rules we felt we could never quite measure up. In particular, we felt we could not always please Uncle Eddie and worried that the smallest infraction (such as putting one shoe on the other which could scuff it) might arouse Uncle Ed's ire.

To be a twin meant having fun. People always had trouble telling us apart and so we depended on each other. For example, Richie had trouble tying his necktie so Bobby tied it for him before traipsing off to school at St. Joseph's elementary school, which catered to the children of Slovak immigrants. Bobby, born five minutes earlier than Richie, became the take-charge person. Richie found contentment in looking up to his older brother for leadership. When we were given I.Q. tests we both scored the same. Bobby scored higher on the quantitative level, but Richie scored higher in terms of verbal intelligence. The combined scores came out to be the same.

Sometimes we received presents both of us could share. On our eighth birthday we received a small, yellow plastic radio bank in which we could store our change. Nowadays most kids would be horrified with such a small gift, particularly one they had to share with their sibling. It was not worth more than a dollar or two, but it had symbolic value for us. It meant that someone cared for us enough to give us a present, however small. We treasured the bank and loved to open it to see how much we had saved.

In fact, we learned to be very thrifty. We collected dirty soda bottles for penny redemption and soon pennies turned into nickels, dimes, quarters, and, yes, dollar bills. They were carefully stuffed into our small, faded yellow radio bank After about a year's time we had saved $50 and we donated that money to be sent to the poor children in Africa.

After about a two-year stay at the Lipinskis' house, we were asked to leave because Aunt Helen took sick and had to spend time in the hospital. Uncle Ed told my Dad that he had to find another place for us since it was too much for Aunt Helen to take care of us. We vividly remember when Aunt Helen went to the hospital to be put in traction to correct a neck problem. She gave us a hug and kiss. This made our day.

As we recall our life then seemed too regimented. This had less to do with the Lipinskis than with the pre-Vatican II church which tended to be rigid and unbending. God seemed like a tough taskmaster, someone we could never please. Although only seven years old, we went to confession once a week, though we really had no sins to confess. We had to memorize the catechism at St. Joseph's Elementary School, which we attended from second to eighth grade. We used to kid around asking, "How do you save your soul?" Answer: "by walking on your heels."

We took our faith very seriously. We were struck by the words of St. Matthew's Gospel, "What does it profit a person to have the whole world and suffer the loss of one's immortal soul." We understood salvation as something we did, avoiding mortal sin, rather than as something done to us, that is, God's grace. The entire elementary school, some 300 children, marched into church every day of the year, Monday through Friday, to attend Mass before school began. The nuns did an outstanding job of keeping hundreds of kids relatively quiet during Mass, although there were occasional snickering and punches exchanged with the boy next to you, when the good Sisters were not looking. We were herded into church on every Friday during Lent to make the Stations of the Cross, which lasted about a good half-hour. To this day we hate making the Stations of the Cross.

The nuns were very strict but had warm hearts. Sr. Edwardina, the principal, though tiny, had a reputation for toughness. She was about to hit an eighth grader who was over six feet tall, when he jumped out an open window to escape her. No one dared get in her way. But Sr. Edwardina turned out to be our guardian angel. She saw to it that we got to go to summer camp. There we could swim and take part in all kinds of fun activities on a lake in northern New Jersey near Newton.

She thought that we twins were too thin and undernourished. She insisted that we have milk every day in the afternoon. We were embarrassed and drank the milk quickly without making this special treatment evident to our classmates. One day she asked us if we would like to become priests. We leaped at the idea. She suggested that we consider joining the Conventual Franciscans since they helped out at our church.

We also got to know the priests well at St. Joseph's. Father Frye and Father Eugene Boneski were assigned there immediately after ordination. St. Joe's turned out to be a great parish in which to cut one's teeth as a minister of God. The people were generous to the clergy and warm-hearted. Father Frye befriended us in part because as an orphan himself had a soft spot for those who were poor and underprivileged.

A MINOR MIRACLE

Dad did not know what to do with us after we were asked to leave the Lipinskis. We visited an orphanage in Newark one Sunday afternoon. On the way back we went to a Catholic church. Dad told us that if we attentively prayed six Our Father's and six Hail Mary's, our prayer requests would be granted. Of course we prayed fervently that we would not have to be put in an orphanage. We then found out what it meant to be helped by an angel. Before we could be sent to the orphanage, Dora Bolger, Dad's first cousin, heard of our plight and decided to take us into her home. Looking back we can categorically say that this must have been a very gutsy move on her part. At the time she had five children of her own, a dog, Trooper, two cats, and two parakeets living in a four bedroom flat with no central heating. We felt that our prayers had been answered.

THE BOLGERS

When we arrived at the Bolgers in the summer of 1949 we were convinced that God had worked a major miracle. The Bolgers lived upstairs in a cold flat at 20 East 28th Street, the other side of the tracks, where life seemed gentler and kinder than on Prospect Avenue. We had no hot water and the rent amounted to $20 a month. That first day, we twins sat down on a big sofa and Dad introduced Cousin Dora and Cousin Joe to us. We were instructed to call them "Cousin" and not simply by their first names. The Bolgers had everything: a dog named Trooper, complete with an ear-piercing bark, two cats, one named Rusty; a large fish tank, a parakeet that would, on occasion, fly the coop and send the household into a panic with the dog and cats desperately trying to get a piece of the bird; and over a hundred comic books, more than the number that existed in the rest of the known world, according to two eight-year-old boys.

The Bolgers had several bikes, both men's and women's, which we were free to ride, an unpaved basketball court in the backyard with a hoop constructed out of a wooden basket, and, best of all, a dozen boys our age, who formed a neighborhood gang. Several boys stand out, Tommy Kavula a terrific athlete who would star in baseball and basketball at Xavier High, a military prep school in Manhattan, and his brother, Bobby, who ran cross-country at Xavier, who usually associated with an older crowd. Tommy died when just 29 years old, killed by a truck driver, high on Bennies or uppers near the

Elizabeth exit (Exit 13) on the New Jersey Turnpike. Their cousin, Johnny Kavula, became our best friend, along with Gregory Varhol known to us only as "Penguin," much to the consternation of his family, who insisted on calling him Gregory. We well remember Joey Corvino, the biggest kid on the block who loved to play tackle football with no padding, in part, because he was more likely to inflict damage on others than get injured himself.

We were not a rebellious gang, although two of the boys made a zip-gun that could fire a single bullet. They made the zip-gun from the aerial of a police car they had broken off. Most of our gang frowned upon this kind of behavior. Our talk consisted of who was the best baseball player, Mickey Mantle or the "Say-Hey" kid, Willie Mays. We did pull some stunts, like climbing in the window at City Hall at noon to get a drink of water or building a tree house, where one of our gang heaved heavy Coke bottles on other kids who tried to take over our tree house.

At times we would have races through the neighbors' yards, climbing over fences and eluding their dogs just for the sheer fun of it. Occasionally, we would take in the Saturday matinee movie and stand in line saying the guy in back has the ticket, which he did, just one for himself, and the other seven of us would break for an open seat. If caught by the usher and expelled from the theatre, we would go downstairs to play pool so our parents would not suspect anything when we came home early from the matinee movie.

We would also have races in the movie under the seats. This proved to be mildly upsetting to those who were more intent on watching the movie and less interested in the race taking place under their very seat. One time at the Saturday matinee Johnny Kavula got a sling shot and with a small rock hit the bull's eye perfectly on a large wall clock in the movie theatre. The ushers were outraged, but we managed to duck under our seats before we could be found out. On another occasion, Bobby won a Flash Gordon gun, highly prized by the rest of our gang.

LA DOLCE VITA

Since the Bolgers had no central heating and no air conditioning at their flat on East 28th Street, to take a bath two options presented themselves. One could boil water on the stove in the kitchen, the emotional center of the house, or one could use the water jacket in the stove to heat the water. Pipes were connected to a water jacket inside the stove. When water got hot inside the stove it went automatically into the boiler or holding tank connected to it. However, the water in the tank could get so hot that one had to open the hot water faucet to let the steam out since there was no release valve on the tank itself. This could be mighty dangerous. If one did not let out the boiling water, the pressure built up inside the boiler by the steam could burst the pipes and send boiling water all over the kitchen. Anyone in the kitchen at the time would get a serious burn.

The stove itself would get so hot that the lids would turn cherry red and Cousin Dora would occasionally bake pancakes on the top. Sometimes Paulie and Vinnie would splash some drops of water on top of the stove and watch the drops dance around until they evaporated. At other times they would surreptitiously take some sawdust or sugar, open the lid, and throw it on top of the glowing coals and watch it explode. For some strange reason they never did this in sight of Cousin Dora. Cousin Dora used to put orange peels on top and the scent would pervade the entire house. If one took a match, held it about two inches away from the peels, then squeezed the peels, oil would drop out and would ignite in a huge flame on top of the stove. Again my cousins did this only if no adult were around to "enjoy" the spectacle.

The story about the stove would be incomplete without mentioning the paraphernalia connected with the stove. Sorry the person who messed with any of these accoutrements connected with the stove. That meant they were in deep trouble. One needed a lid handle to lift the cast iron lids on top of the stove and a poker to gently move wood and coal to the center of the fire. A crank served to jiggle the dead ashes down from the grates, while a long, thin shovel could be used to remove ashes from the stove to be put in a pail until they cooled. The ashes were then either strewn all over the yard or thrown into the garbage can. The garbage collectors had to lift these extremely heavy garbage cans into an open truck. To accomplish this herculean task, they had to be the strongest persons in the entire city.

The stove feasted on both wood and coal. However, the coal gave off more heat than the wood. Vinnie took charge of the wood. He cut it using a two person saw called a "To Me to You Saw," which one pulled and never pushed. After chopping the wood, Vinnie placed it in the shed to keep it dry. From there Vinnie put it into peach baskets, which were stored on the covered steps leading from the backyard to the flat upstairs. One day, in fact, Vinnie went down the back stairs and tripped. He managed to come tumbling down the stairs first, followed by six baskets of wood and six pails of coal. Luckily, his winter clothes acted as padding and he arose shaken to the bone, but not seriously hurt, except for minor cuts and bruises. Strangely, from then on he, understandably, used only the front stairs of the flat.

After Paulie left home to join the Air Force, we twins helped Vinnie with the wood. He showed us how to use an axe without mangling our toes and let us take turns helping him cut wood with the two person saw. In all of this Vinnie proved to be the soul of patience with us, particularly when we tried to push the saw rather than pull it. We were never cold in winter but in the dog days of summer our bedroom could get real hot even with every window open and with a large fan running on high in our bedroom.

The flat had neither a regular bathtub, nor a shower. All the kids got their baths in a soapstone wash tub about four feet long, two feet wide and one and a half feet deep. The Bolger children, most of who were in their teens at the time we were there, also took their bath there once a week, except for Cousin Joe and Cousin Dora. Cousin Joe took his shower at work while Dora went to the Gala house where they had a huge bathtub, large enough to accommodate an adult six feet tall. At times, the Bolger children were given the opportunity to go to the Galas for a real bath.

Trooper, the beloved family dog, also got washed in this tub, after coming home stinking to high heaven because he roamed the neighborhood for a couple of days during mating season. Rectangular in shape this wash tub was used along with a wringer washing machine to rinse out our clothes. Most of the time it had a cover and the everyday dishes were kept there after they were washed in the sink.

Paulie, Vinnie, and we twins shared one bedroom, while Dora, her husband, Joe, and their youngest daughter, Doris, shared the other. We did have bed bugs but we could not feel them. They just took some blood from us at night. No big deal. In those days many families had both bed bugs and roaches. We had a code name for the roaches. We called the roaches "friends."

The middle daughters, Margie and Irene, shared a fold-up bed which had to be wheeled into the living room each evening. As teenagers this must have strained their privacy. Further, this portable bed must have been uncomfortable and quite small for two persons, yet Irene and Margie never complained. Tempers might flare a bit in the morning around 7:30 when nine people had to use the bathroom before leaving for either work or school, particularly when one or two of us were running late. However, the Bolgers were quite civil to each other living in such close quarters and conflicts were practically non-existent.

THE MAGIC OF CHRISTMAS

Dora Bolger had a brother, John, who never married, universally known as "Uncle Johnny." He usually helped get our Christmas tree. Of course we had a real tree and after picking it out he would come in the house to set it up. First, the bottom had to be cut off and made flat; second, he would drill holes into the empty areas and insert other limbs to turn it into a real prize tree. Next, he would put on the lights, after which Doris and we twins would put on the tinsel very meticulously, one individual strand after the other. If we just threw on the tinsel we were gently told to shape up.

The Bolgers celebrated Christmas in a spectacular way. In the weeks prior to Christmas we twins and Doris would save up our money and go shopping together on Broadway to buy small gifts for every member of the Bolger family. Cousin Dora gave us hints on what we should buy. And Doris knew where. It was fun to think of inventive places to hide the gifts in a house that had no room to spare. The presents also had to be "snuck" into the house surreptitiously without arousing the suspicion of the adults. Happily, we were never caught.

Gifts were exchanged on Christmas Eve when we were treated to a special dinner. Festivities began with a prayer. At times, Cousin Joe would say a spontaneous prayer and lose his train of thought and one could hear little snickers of laughter around the table. Cousin Dora made mushroom soup, which we hated but tried not to show it, followed by the main course of fish and spaghetti. We also had *oplatky,* a type of wafer found in Slovak and Polish parishes, made especially for Christmas. The *oplatky* was dipped in honey and passed around the table on a small plate. Think of it as a kind of communion bread. When passed around the table we felt the closeness the Apostles must have experienced at the Last Supper. The Bolgers then sang Christmas carols in Slovak and in English. After fifty years we still remember some of the tunes.

After dinner we exchanged gifts. What a thrill because we never knew what we would get. We were never once disappointed. And we were always surprised. We usually received cuff links or clothes, which we could then wear to midnight Mass and feel like a million dollars. One Christmas Paulie gave us shaving cream and a shaver. We were 16 at the time and really treasured that gift. Then we went to midnight Mass where we served as altar boys.

On Christmas Day itself the magic continued. We would go to Cousin Johnny's house and he always had something special for Doris and us twins. One Christmas Doris received a bicycle and we received a golden watch that shone like the sun. Out of sheer joy, we cried. Another Christmas Johnny gave us a camera, complete with flash, which we loved. For us and the Bolger children, Uncle Johnny seemed to be the incarnation of Santa Claus himself. Johnny would also give us tons of colored paper he would get free from the printing factory where he worked in Manhattan.

SUMMER FUN

During the summers we spent part of our vacation at Johnny's summer place in Pine Lake Park, located about five miles from Toms River, New Jersey.

He had bought some land there on which he built a house. When we first laid our eyes on the property, it reminded us of the wilderness. It overflowed with scores of trees and bushes. The men first made an outhouse, which also served as a cache for the tools needed to build a house from scratch. Uncle Johnny taught us how to row a boat with oars and trusted us to take the boat out by ourselves with a 5 horsepower Evinrude motor, which made enough noise to rival that of a 5,000 horsepower engine.

Uncle Johnny's home sat on a man-made lake and we took the boat up the tributary to go fishing. We sometimes caught pickerel and then barbecued them for supper. One time, while swimming near a patch of lily weeds, a fish slipped into Bob's swimsuit. This caused him to exit the water in panicky mode. How affirming to have a male like Uncle Johnny in our lives, particularly one so generous with his time and his money. It made the world seem less harsh for us.

One year we were treated to a two week vacation in Connecticut. Unfortunately, we had three flat tires on the way. Tires in those days were poorly constructed and folks often had a flat tire. One of the tires simply burst before we got started, because the car had seven passengers and a heavy load of food and clothing. Ray Innella drove us there on the Merritt Parkway in Connecticut and Vinnie drove us home in a Nash. The Nash would overheat in the summer if one went over fifty miles an hour, and would konk out in the winter, if one went under fifty miles an hour. Strange but true.

We spent eight wonderful years with the Bolgers. Our great passion at the time involved playing all kinds of games and collecting trivial items such as bottle caps, which we collected from Al's candy store on the corner of Broadway and 28th Street, leather heels from the shoemaker, and baseball cards. Little did we know back then that those baseball cards would someday be worth a small fortune. The heels were used to play a game in which we used chalk to divide the street into four corner boxes with one large circle in the middle. One had to land a heel in the box without touching any of the chalk edges. To this day we have never seen anyone play this game except the kids on 28th Street in Bayonne during the early 1950s.

We did not eschew the traditional games of baseball, basketball, and football, which we played on the lawn of City Hall and 30th Street. But we also had our non-traditional games, such as stickball played in the streets with manhole covers serving as home plate and second base respectively. We played this game with a pink rubber ball that could be easily seen if smashed into the neighbor's front-lawn garden and a thin stick that we took off an old mop. Sometimes when one of us hit the ball into a neighbor's yard we never saw it again. Some residents cut the ball in two in order to express their indignation that the ball landed on their property. This did absolutely nothing to deter us from playing stickball in the street.

We also played king of the hill, the aim of which was to stay on top of the hill as others tried to wrestle one to the ground, and diamond ball, which we played at the back entrance of Frank Kavula's tavern and restaurant. In this game one had to hit a ball with the hand into the boxes that were formed when the entrance way was constructed. Another game bore the name, Ring-a-Lario, a modified version of tag. The person who was "it" had to touch another kid on the head long enough to bellow out "One, two, three Ring-a-lario."

MASS AT HOME

When we were about ten years old we pretended to say Mass at home in Cousin Dora's bedroom. Doris Bolger also joined in helping us find suitable vestments from the clothes we had and could borrow from other members of the household. We turned an ordinary drinking cup into a chalice and a dresser into an altar. We did this very respectfully because we did not think it right to fool around and laugh in "church." We took turns playing the part of the celebrant. The other two acted as acolytes.

We were very happy at the Bolgers. We played until we were ready to drop, going to bed each night bone-tired and sleeping like rocks. The Bolgers treated us as family and never scrimped on food. Potatoes sold for a nickel a pound and Cousin Dora loved to buy fresh fruit from the street peddler, particularly grapes, watermelon in the summer, and her favorite, Bing cherries from the peddler. Cousin Dora would send us to the grocery store for small items like milk and butter. One time she sent us to Mrs. Bissel's store to buy lunch meat. Mrs. Bissel could not stop laughing out loud and she told us why. The previous customer, a young newlywed, came into the store asking to buy Elbow Grease. Her young husband had told her to use it in cleaning and she thought that it was a type of product.

Cousin Joe liked to eat goulash, a Slovak stew, but we twins only ate lean meat. We were only too glad to give any fatty meat to the dog, Trooper, waiting for our quick hand under the table. Trooper had enough doggy wisdom to be in the right spot at the right time. Never once did Trooper betray our confidence. How we loved that dog's ability to keep our secret. Cousin Dora, a fantastic cook, knew how to make the most of leftovers. We experienced Cousin Dora to be a simple person with a heart as big as the State of Alaska. She had tremendous energy. She managed a family of nine while working part-time at a sewing factory located one hundred feet from our flat. She worked to earn what she termed, "pin money." In retrospect, we marveled at her ability to pull this off so well, that is, managing work and home. Many years later, when Richie got his Ph.D. from the University of Munich, she stated in her homespun way, "Richie, you turned out smart."

MARIST HIGH SCHOOL

After graduating from St. Joseph's Elementary School we wanted to go directly to the seminary in Staten Island run by the Conventual Franciscans. But because they only accepted students entering tenth grade, we went to Marist High School, a new school opened by the Marist Brothers on 8th Street and the Boulevard. It was the first year of operation for the school, which consisted of a series of homes converted into classrooms. Brother Leo Sylvius served as the principal and taught us Latin.

Some of the students came from Jersey City. Brother Robert, who taught History, served as Richie's homeroom teacher. The brothers were superb teachers and knew how to instill the fear of God into us. If one got out of line Brother Robert could, on occasion, come down to the offender's desk, carefully remove his watch, and slap the student in the face. This kind of intimidation worked very effectively, thank you.

If on Monday morning one's homework assignments were not completed, Brother Robert would order the slackers go into a small room off the classroom. They were then asked to take off their suit jacket, bend down, and be paddled with a ruler or small stick. Strangely enough, by the end of the first month of class very few students would come to school on Monday morning without their homework assignment in hand.

At the end of ninth grade we went off to the seminary, leaving Bayonne for good, except for summer vacations. Dad and Grandma Penaskovic had tremendous respect for the clergy and were delighted by our decision to enter. Dad, though, had always told us to do what we wanted and put absolutely no pressure on us. We felt called by God to become priests and that's the basic reason why we entered the seminary. One single event does not mark the end of childhood, but the move from Bayonne to the seminary in Staten Island marked the end of our early youth.

COUNTING OUR BLESSINGS

1. We learned that God could be found in times of trouble. Although we may experience wind and storms, disruption, and separation, God might be compared to the sun on a cloudy day. God's there all right, but her presence is hidden. We would like to feel the warm rays of the sun but must be content with the knowledge that God is there the entire time playing peek-a-boo behind the clouds. This implies that faith rules. We now see but darkly, but then in the hereafter, we shall see face to face.

2. We were taught to be extremely grateful for small things, like a plastic radio bank. We knew that the thought behind the gift is more precious than the gift itself.

3. We felt God's gently, caressing hand guiding us throughout our lives as children, for example, the very fact that the Lipinski and Bolger families took us in and genuinely cared for us. Our lives might have turned out quite differently if we had been raised in an orphanage. Both Aunt Helen and Cousin Dora forgot that they did not actually give birth to us. Instead, they treated us like their own children. For that we'll be indebted for all eternity.

4. It's amazing that Bob and I turned out to be normal and well put together, psychologically and emotionally speaking, despite two strikes against us. First, we had to endure the break-up of our family when we were young, and second, we had to overcome the disposition to mental illness in our genes. How we survived and flourished as adults remains incomprehensible to us. Perhaps we were touched by God?

Chapter Three

The Long Hand of Providence

"I knew that my vocation was found. I had received the call, and having done so I was sure my work would be assigned me. Of some things we feel quite certain. Inside there is a click, a kind of bell that strikes, when the hands of our destiny meet at the meridian hour."

Amelia E. Barr

"Our real journey in life is interior: it is a matter of growth, deepening, and of an ever greater surrender to the creative action of love and grace in our hearts."

Thomas Merton

How did it happen that a set of twins from an obscure city in New Jersey would one day have their picture snapped with the Pope in St. Peter's Basilica in Rome? How did it happen that Bobby Brown would one day have a successful practice in psychotherapy while Richie Blue would be a full professor at a major university in the United States? How did it happen that the twins would both wind up marrying former nuns, both of whom were registered nurses working in hospital administration? Was this destiny? Divine Providence? Or something else?

Informed by particle physics, cosmology, and modern astrophysics, scientists today speak about the Anthropic Principle. This principle says that it appears that the universe is such that it's marked by values of the basic constants that are precisely those necessary for our existence. It suggests that the world seems to be finely-tuned with respect to many physical features in a way conducive to the emergence of living organisms and hence of human beings. The presence of humans in the cosmos represents an inbuilt potentiality of that physical universe in the sense that self-conscious, intelligent life was bound to appear.

We believe that the Anthropic Principle applies in a sense to our lives as twins. The conditions in our life were such that entering the seminary seemed to follow naturally. As altar servers we came to admire the priests with whom we came into contact. We both were idealistic young men with a keen desire to change the world in a positive way. What better way than by enlisting in the service of the Almighty? Thanks to a higher power, we both felt called to the service of God in the Franciscan Order. We saw it as God's plan for us.

When we made the joint decision to enter the Franciscan Order, we knew that we had each other. It would have been very difficult to live apart at that time. Although our family had a history of mental illness, we discovered that we could carry on as a result of the emotional bond that existed between us. We also knew from experience that it's not difficult to hang on by a thread, provided God holds the other end. Looking back, God had a hand in our lives, starting off with our birth and continuing down the labyrinthine ways that constitute our lives.

STATEN ISLAND

Our hearts beat fast and a sense of excitement coursed through our veins as we ascended the eight stairs to the main entrance of St. Francis Seminary. Dad and our cousin, Irene Innella, and her husband, Ray, drove us to the seminary. Irene and Ray sensed that we were rather young (we were fifteen) to enter the seminary, yet if that's what we wanted, who were they to say otherwise?

Why did we enter? We had felt called to the priesthood ever since we were seven years old and, in fact, would have joined the Franciscans as freshmen in high school, but they did not accept ninth graders. We particularly liked the Conventual Franciscans because they seemed so human and down-to-earth.

Most people think of the Franciscans as one order when, in reality, there are three main branches. There's the Order of Friars Minor or "the Brownies" so-called because they wear a brown habit. On the other hand, the Conventual Franciscans wear a black habit (or in some countries a grey habit). Then there's the Capuchins, who broke off from the Conventual Franciscans. The Capuchins wear a pointed cowl (capuche), sandals, and a beard. The Capuchins are the strictest branch. We did not know the differences between the three branches when we joined the Conventual Franciscans.

We chose the Conventuals because we had gotten to know them upfront and personally since they said Mass at our church in Bayonne, St. Joseph's.

And we had toured St. Francis in eighth grade and were taken with Father Dunstan Mc Dermott, who had a terrific sense of humor. The seminary's proximity to Bayonne was another factor in our decision to enter: we could take a ferry from Bayonne to Staten Island, take a bus from Port Richmond to the foot of Victory Boulevard, and make the steep climb up Todt Hill Road to the seminary.

To us the Conventual Franciscans were a cut above the diocesan priests we had known. We put in an application to enter the seminary and in the summer of 1955 received a letter from Father Colman Mc Greevey congratulating us on our acceptance into St. Francis. Surprisingly, we never discussed our reasons for entering the seminary with each other. We took for granted that this is what we wanted to do with our lives, i.e., become priests.

The seminary, though only a half-hour ride from our home in Bayonne, New Jersey distance-wise, may as well have been on another planet. Bayonne then and now might best be characterized as a blue-collar town. Thousands of men and women worked for the Esso Standard Oil Company. Houses were often flush next to each other or separated by a yard or less. Only three miles long and about one mile wide, Bayonne in those days had a population of about 76,000. The streets were often clogged with traffic, particularly on Avenue E where a stream of large trucks paraded in and out of the city.

Back in the Fifties, Staten Island, easily more than ten times the size of Bayonne, had a relatively sparse population compared to the other boroughs of New York City. In the early Fifties the Verrazano Bridge connecting Staten Island to Brooklyn had not yet been built, and one could travel through large stretches of the Island and encounter few cars and fewer people.

St. Francis, the minor seminary of the Conventual Franciscans of the Immaculate Conception Province sat on the highest point of the eastern seaboard of the United States in a secluded section of the Island, Todt Hill, where today only the wealthy can afford to live. The setting of St. Francis surprised us both at the time with its idyllic, rich, green foliage, spacious grounds, well-kept lawns, a private pond for fishing or ice hockey, clay tennis courts that were easy on the feet, a baseball field that could double for flag football, woods for hiking, and, above all, complete privacy. The main building exudes majesty, made entirely of stone and solid bricks. Its carefully designed lines bespeak strength, the entire setting an emblem of quiet power and majesty. The building itself remains a forceful reminder of another dimension in life, the spiritual. Compared to the asphalt jungle of Bayonne, the seminary and its grounds seemed like the Shangri-La.

A MICROCOSM OF THE WORLD

St. Francis functioned indeed as a world unto itself with its own agenda, goals, and rules. There we, twins, learned to swim freely in one of the great wisdom traditions, that of the Conventual Franciscans. Wisdom for us meant knowledge plus virtue. In the final analysis wisdom exists as a gift of God, grace if you will. Like Isaiah and Jeremiah we felt unworthy, yet we were called to this way of life by a voice from above. To this day St. Francis Seminary remains for us hallowed ground. We feel God speaks to humanity loudly via the ups and downs of daily life.

We entered the seminary with a fragile sense of self. In many families parents dole out praise on a regular basis to their children. Our Mom lived apart from us in a mental hospital and could not be there for us beyond our sixth birthday. The same held true for Dad, who lived with our younger siblings, Tom and Bill, in the home of our grandparents. Of course we visited Dad on most weekends but only for a few hours. We lacked the daily interaction with our parents that most children take for granted. This probably affected out self-concept understood as a mental blueprint of who we are. However, by adhering to the regimen of the seminary and under the watchful eyes of the Franciscan Fathers, who were effectively our surrogate parents, we found that we could compete with our peers intellectually, athletically, and emotionally. We found that we could do a great deal in all areas and do it well. This "can-do" attitude remained for us throughout our lives.

A spiritual director differs from a counselor and a psychotherapist. Spiritual direction itself cannot be reduced to a set of life skills taught by a social worker, nor is it catechetical training. A spiritual director is a mature fellow Christian who helps one grow in the spiritual life. At St. Francis each seminarian had a spiritual director. Back in 1956, Richie received spiritual direction from Father Venard, a gem of a human being whose compassion rivaled that of a Zen Buddhist monk.

Our spiritual directors in the Franciscan tradition had the task of helping us come closer to God and gave us prayerful guidance in the struggle to discern the presence of God in our lives. They would inquire about our prayer life, uncover the wealth of spiritual graces hidden in our routine daily chores, and allow us to see opportunities for growth in what may have appeared to be only obstacles. They taught us to do spiritual reading, suggesting a life of St. Francis by Cuthbert or Jorgensen or various other books.

We were homesick the first six weeks of school but simultaneously buoyed up by the friendliness of the friars and our classmates. There were only ten students in our sophomore class, two of whom left at the end of the year. Latin and geometry were our most difficult subjects. Sports were emphasized and we became pack rats in the basketball gym. We played intramural flag football, basketball, and baseball. We became good athletes and eventually made the high school varsity basketball and baseball teams. Later, we made the junior varsity baseball and basketball teams in junior college.

We joined the choir as altos. Our voices had a particular strength and beauty before they broke. By the end of our junior year in high school we had become hoarse-throated adolescents, singing second bass.

We were very short, 5 feet, 2 inches tall as sophomores but then sprouted to 5 feet, 9 inches for Richie and 5 feet, 11 for Bobby. We weighed a mere 125 pounds but ate like horses. Bobby helped the German sisters in the kitchen, hauling supplies from the storeroom such as 100 pound bags of flour and sugar. He got rewarded handsomely with extra food and dessert, some of which he passed on to Richie and close friends such as Russ Siller.

MIRROR IMAGES

People constantly got us confused because we were mirror images of each other. Bobby wrote with his right hand and batted and threw lefty. Richie wrote with his left hand and hit and threw righty. Bobby had an excellent set shot in basketball; Richie had a two-hand jump shot. One time we played a visiting team in basketball. They got us confused. They were looking for Bobby to take a two-hand jump shot and Richie for a long set shot. We scored a lot of points on that particular day. We both loved ping-pong and took turns becoming the best players in the school in the annual tournament.

We were the only set of twins in the seminary and that made us special. In the refectory where we took our meals, six students were assigned to a particular table. We would, on occasion, sit in each other's seat just for the fun of it. The Prefect of Students, Father Timothy Lyons, never noticed the switch, much to our relief. If he had noticed he would have been upset and it would have been particularly embarrassing to Bobby, who cleaned Father Tim's room each morning. Father Timothy also asked Bobby to run the 50–50 program, set up to raise money for the seminary, and Fr. Tim employed both of us in the summers to give out Mass cards to those requesting them and to perform other secretarial duties. Bobby became such a fixture in this capacity that the members of the 50–50 club paid the cost of making our habits and bought us breviaries as we moved on to the novitiate in Middleburg, New York.

CONVENTUAL WISDOM

What wisdom did we learn from the Franciscans? The Conventual Franciscans taught us to take an upbeat, optimistic view of life. They were very human, that is, they were approachable and down-to-earth, possessed a terrific sense of humor, and were humble to boot. The Conventual friars also gave us "enlargement of mind." This capacity, the very opposite of prejudice and bigotry, involved the expansion of the mind and came about in a two-fold way: First, it was the direct consequence of an education in the liberal arts, such as the books we read such as Zenophon's *Anabasis* in Greek, Virgil's *Aeneid* in Latin, and the plays of Victor Hugo read in French under the watchful eyes of Father Kenan Mc Gowan. Second, the Franciscan friars, particularly Father Gervase, modeled this behavior themselves and we took our cues from them.

THE FACULTY

The friars did not always set out to teach us wisdom directly. Much of what we learned rubbed off from them by a kind of osmosis. We remember listening, for example, to classical music, which emanated from the room of Father Reynold Kowalski, who blared it throughout the third floor of the building. We heard Tchaikovsky and Mozart for the first time and became enthralled with classical music. To this day both of us find classical music soothing to our inner spirit, an oasis in the desert of daily life.

We regard Father Reynold as the first bona fide intellectual we encountered. He reveled in the life of the mind, reading voraciously, the epitome of a littérateur. He introduced us to the poetry of Gerard Manley Hopkins, William Butler Yeats, and T.S. Eliot. He played recordings of T.S. Eliot and other greats in class and even read to us some of his own poetry.

Father Kenan Mc Gowan impressed us because of his very relaxed approach to life. From his exterior one would not guess that here stood a man of profound spirituality, a savvy basketball coach, and mentor. He had the patience of Job and very few things in life really threw him for a loss. He played well the hand he was dealt, and, for that reason, served as a wisdom figure for us. He possessed a terrific sense of humor and used understatement effectively. As an example of his wry humor he could say with a straight face, "Do I have to stand on my head to illustrate a point?"

Father Kenan functioned as a surrogate father figure for us. He called Richie "Junior" (since Bobby was older by five minutes) to distinguish him from Bobby. To this day he remains one of our heroes. In fact, Richie named his middle child Kenan after Father Kenan.

We had oodles of respect for Father Gervase Beyer, teacher, *par excellence*. He taught us logic, Latin, and persuasive speech. He read widely in the areas of the natural sciences, literature, and philosophy and he felt as comfortable talking about Heisenberg's Uncertainty Principle as he did about Antoine de Saint Exupery's book *Wind, Sand, and the Stars*. Gervase could harpoon a person to the wall with his tongue and trenchant wit: "Penaskovic, I'll flunk you so low a pancake will look like the Empire State Building." "Mr. Brown, you won't have to come up for your grade. I'll roll it down to you."

Father Gervase's take on John Donne's famous line "No man is an island" went like this: "Every man is an island with at most a leaky rowboat." He peppered his lectures with such maxims as "You never graduate from human nature," and "No one has a monopoly on wisdom," or conversely "No one has a monopoly on stupidity." Father Gervase encouraged us to think for ourselves, paraphrasing the dictum of Aquinas, "Don't quote what the authorities have said about a subject, but consider the truth of the matter yourself."

Father Gervase had an enormous impact on our intellectual development. He encouraged us to read widely in a wide variety of fields, including the natural sciences, philosophy, and fiction. Gervase might be dubbed the incarnation of the "Renaissance" man. He sounded gruff in class but deep down possessed a soft heart. He enjoyed kidding others and appreciated students like Dick Shields who could stand toe-to-toe with him and trade insults. Unfortunately, Father Gervase or "Gerry" died of cancer at an early age. Of all the professors we ever had both in the U.S. and abroad he was *facile princeps*, or easily the best.

Timothy Lyons, Prefect of Discipline, served as another wisdom figure for us. He had an uncanny knack of sizing people up, combined with a strong prayer life that sustained him. Of sterling character he combined an even-going temperament with deep insight into human nature. He knew when to be stern and when to bend. Tim, endowed by the Almighty with megatons of common sense, had a very strong sense of fairness. He loved to win, be it playing ping-pong or basketball, but took losing graciously. Tim liked to engage in verbal repartee and could do battle with the best of us. He had an excellent vocabulary, developed from spending long hours doing crossword puzzles which completely fascinated him. This no-nonsense friar taught by example.

Father Tim gave us lessons on etiquette, telling us how often we were to change our socks and underwear. He wanted us to be cultured gentlemen down to our fingernails, *ad unquem*, as the Latin phrase puts it. Father Tim kept a close eye on us from his room which faced out into the study hall. Some wag named his room, the front of which consisted almost entirely of glass, the fish bowl. From this vantage-point he could stare at us with his so-called "glass eye." Tim struck us as a take-charge person, witty, likeable, and, above all, fair. He did not play favorites. We thought of him, if it's not blasphemous to say, as the human counterpart to God the Father: wise, compassionate, and just.

Father Tim did have his faults. He told Richie to quit his summer job as an orderly in St. Vincent's Hospital. One of the nurses was attracted to Richie and held his hand as they were walking down the hall of the hospital. In his naiveté Richie mentioned this to Father Tim, who counseled Richie to quit the job immediately for the sake of his vocation. Father Tim meant well but it might have been better if Richie's vocation were tested at that time by life in the real world.

Father Sebastian Weber served as rector of the seminary. Students affectionately called him "Sebby Weber." Known to be a "tough cookie," little wonder that we had a song that went, "Tell me why, there's no sun up in the sky, Sebby Weber." As a student at the major seminary in Rome on San Teodoro Street he could not stand the body odor of the Italians. One day at morning prayer he used a can of room freshener to fumigate the friar from Italy in front of him, much to the consternation of the other Italian friars, who were outraged by this "Americano." Little wonder that they called for his expulsion, but to no avail.

We sensed a feeling of camaraderie among the priests and brothers at St. Francis Seminary. Based on our thoughtful assessment of them, they possessed a genuine respect and liking for one another. They were men of deep thought and profound spirituality. As human beings they were well put together, emotionally speaking. They also embodied the basic qualities of Franciscan spirituality: humility, compassion for the downtrodden, generosity, and detachment from material things. These committed men were impressive without trying to be so. Their actions spoke much louder than their words.

OTHER SEMINARIANS

The minor seminary taught us that wisdom's lessons are best learned through a wise community of the heart. The entire community at St. Francis Seminary served as God's instrument in teaching us wisdom. From the hundreds who applied to the seminary only about sixty were selected for admission. We were a young, idealistic group of men with quick minds and a sincere desire to serve the Lord as friars following St. Francis, our founder. True, we had our share of oddballs and characters but they, thank you very much, did not last. They either left voluntarily or were shown the exit door.

The seminary had high admission standards. One had to undergo a battery of psychological tests before one could gain admittance. Father Jeffrey Keefe, a clinical psychologist, administered these tests. Throughout our years in the seminary we were warned not to develop a particular friendship, that is, an emotional, exclusive attachment to any one person. We found our colleagues in the seminary to be well-balanced and emotionally healthy human beings. Those who stayed developed an esprit d'corps and camaraderie that time will not sunder.

We were not given advice about dealing with our sexuality either at home or in the seminary. We were expected to learn about the facts of life on our own. This made puberty a difficult time for us. Neither of us could understand the changes that were occurring in our bodies as we became teenagers. We thought that we were losing our minds when sexual thoughts dominated our consciousness.

Yet we managed to come through this difficult period of time unscathed that is, we were able to adjust and accept our sexuality, have a healthy self-concept, and relate well to others. We felt affirmed by the friars and by our colleagues in the seminary. The seminary may have been a hothouse, but it was one that provided all the nutrients for sound emotional growth.

There was a good balance between intellectual pursuits or mental stimulation and athletics. We were encouraged to sublimate our sexual energy by playing flag football, basketball, and baseball. We were challenged both on the athletic field and in the classroom. Our superiors gave us sufficient time to do well in our studies and in developing our own personal prayer life. We spent time in the chapel praying to God, beyond the times we had for formal chapel prayer.

We learned piety from the two Anthonys, Tony Gigliotti, our classmate, a gentle soul from Carbondale, Pennsylvania, and Antony Magalhaes, a Brazilian, who spent many long hours in the seminary chapel. Both knelt so long in prayer before the statue of Mary that we often wondered if their knees were glued to the kneeler. From the Bostonian with the thick New England accent, Frank Madden, we learned worldly wisdom. F.X., as he was affectionately called, had a storehouse of jokes and anecdotes. F.X. had the Irish gift of blarney and could weave an incredible story, one that seemed to somehow transcend the boundaries of both space and time. He had an effervescent, upbeat spirit sustained by a winning smile.

Barry Angelini, a student from Albany, New York, taught us how to play chess and how to laugh at our own foibles. He had a gift of seeing through any kind of pretense and phoniness combined with a delightful sense of humor. One time he shook a small round plate of Jell-O and asked, "What does this remind you of?" The correct answer, Larry M. (who had a large posterior), at the pencil sharpener. Barry had a sharp mind and a "can-do" attitude toward life. Later on he would be ordained and work for a time as a missionary in Costa Rica and at a high school in Torrance, California, one so tough that it rivaled missionary work.

There were five German sisters from the environs of Wuerzburg, Germany who cooked for us and did the laundry. They were the workhorses of the seminary. They spoke broken English and lived a hard life, rising at 5 A.M. for mediation at 5:30 A.M. They had never seen an athletic supporter before. And when one of the seminarians threw his athletic supporter into the laundry (which we were not to do) he was surprised when it came back, sown carefully into underwear.

Between them, the Conventual Franciscans taught us other, valuable life lessons such as "accentuating the positive." The Franciscans believed strongly in the motto, "Better to light one candle than to curse the darkness." This lesson came home to us in various ways, be it in the retreats given by Father George or Father Conall Mc Hugh or in the spiritual reading we did in regard to things Franciscan. The Franciscans taught us the importance of poverty or detachment. Throughout our lives we have reflected on the words of the Franciscan, Jacopone di Tode who said, "Poverty is to have nothing, to desire nothing, yet to possess everything in the spirit of liberty."

Some qualities such as concern for the poor and less fortunate rubbed off on us twins. Throughout our lives we experienced God by developing in our lives a humanizing solidarity with the poor. Richie found himself looking for a job in 1973 when a homeless person on the streets of San Francisco asked for a handout. Richie saw Christ in that man and took him to a restaurant in the Tenderloin district and treated him to a meal. That action was rooted in the Franciscan emphasis on giving to the less fortunate.

SUMMER EMPLOYMENT

During the summer the minor seminary closed and the students went home. We took various odd jobs during the summer. Bobby's first summer job involved delivering Western Union telegrams by bicycle throughout the city of Bayonne on weekends. The job paid $1 an hour, but the tips were great. Sometimes Bobby would bring home $20 a day in tips, which he would save for Christmas presents for the Bolgers or for vacation. On a particularly good day he might come home hoarse from too much singing. In those days he had, on occasion, to deliver "singing Telegrams." At times, he had to deliver a death announcement in its yellow envelope with black edges.

The hardest part of the job involved delivering telegrams in poor, run-down neighborhoods. Their children would answer the door and invariably let their German shepherd or Doberman pinscher out to lunge at him. To this day Bobby has a great deal of respect for postal workers.

A FAMILY REUNION

Fantasies and daydreams are a part of every child's life. As children we fantasized that our five brothers would one day live under one roof together. This did not occur until the summer of 1957 when Dad leased an apartment at 267 Broadway. We twins were juniors in the seminary at the time and were thrilled to be together with our family. In hindsight one might call it a railroad flat in poor condition, but that did not matter as long as we were all together. Prior to the move we all had a hand in scrapping the old paint off the walls and adding some new paint, an exciting time for all of us.

Downstairs a bar and a loud jukebox constantly played hit tunes like "Volare" until 2 A.M. Our older brother Frank bought a huge Oldsmobile 98 from the money he saved stocking shelves on the night shift at the Acme supermarket near Journal Square in Jersey City. One time Frank happened to be the last one to leave the bowling alley. The Jersey City police stopped him in his tracks and accused him of robbing the bowling alley. They had to let him go after checking his trunk and not finding any burglary tools. Another time the three of us were stopped in Jersey City by the cops, who thought we looked suspicious. They told us to get out of town pronto and go back to Bayonne.

We felt that our ship had come in when Frank bought the car. Now we could go as a family to visit Mom at the county mental hospital in Secaucus without having to take three buses on Sunday afternoon, a trip that could take up to two or three hours. In fact, the bus ride took longer than the time we had to visit Mom.

PORK OR LAMB CHOPS?

One summer Richie worked in a kosher meat market owned by Irving Reitner and his wife. They were a sweet couple and trusted Richie enough to have him go to the bank every few days and make deposits of $500–800 dollars in cash. Every Monday morning the rabbi would come in and inspect the meats to make sure they were indeed in conformity with the Jewish laws for purification. Part of Richie's job consisted of opening and closing the door for the rabbi, who went into the freezer and checked out everything very carefully.

One day Richie made a *faux pas* in front of many waiting customers. He asked Irving, "How much are these pork chops, Mr. Reitner?" The customers sighed in unison and had a terrible look on their faces. Mr. Reitner almost choked when he heard the question and replied, "Richie, you know we don't sell *pork* chops, those are *lamb* chops."

Once Richie struck up a conversation in the home of one of Mr. Reitner's customers. She told Richie he would make a good father some day. Richie thought to himself, "Lady, you're right but I won't be a "father" in the biological sense but in a spiritual sense. As life would have it, both parties were correct.

ON WAXING A RUG

In the summer of 1961 we found employment with Building Services Corporation located at Five Corners in Jersey City, New Jersey, near Journal Square. Our wages were minimal, $1.25 an hour, but the possibility of working overtime to increase our take home pay made the job attractive. The job consisted of washing and waxing floors at banks, offices, and companies located around Hudson County. Our co-workers were ex-convicts, former Marines, unskilled workers with little or no education, the outcasts of society. We stood out from them because we looked so clean-cut. We were even told that by the employees of companies whose offices we cleaned.

One day we asked one of our co-workers what he did for fun. He said, "I drink beer and shoot pool." The job started at 5 P.M. and went until 2 A.M. On Friday we got paid only after the shift was over. It seems that prior to our employment checks were given out before the Friday evening shift, but some of the employees would then go to the gin mill, get pickled, and then wreck the truck. So we all had to return to the office at 2 A.M. to receive our paychecks.

We cleaned the offices of the huge Western Electric plant in Kearney, New Jersey. After cleaning the offices, much to our surprise, we had to step out of the truck and be frisked before leaving the premises. It seems that a few weeks before we were hired one of our 'honorable' co-workers sat on a typewriter in the back of the truck and made off with it before anyone discovered the theft.

One of our co-workers had profound mental problems. He had the job of cleaning the rug in one of the executive suites. Instead of vacuuming the rug, he actually washed and waxed it. Problems arose when he tried to buff the rug, to the profound amazement of the supervisor, who fired him on the spot.

After getting off from work at 2 A.M. we had to catch the bus from Journal Square to Bayonne. The last bus left at 2:30 A.M. One day Richie was running late and decided to sprint the four blocks to Journal Square to catch the last bus. Little did he know that a patrol car followed him to the bus. The police officer escorted him off the bus and accused him of robbing parking meters. Richie showed him his badge from Building Services Corporation. He also emptied out his pockets to show that he did not have a huge amount of coins. The officer let Richie go. When Richie re-entered the bus he felt like a criminal because the police car stationed itself in front of the bus in full view of all the passengers.

BE STILL AS A MOUNTAIN

After graduating from St. Francis minor seminary we were off to the novitiate of the Conventual Franciscans in Middleburg, New York. The novitiate serves as a kind of boot camp for religious life and weeds out those unsuitable for life as a Franciscan. Middleburg is located out in the sticks about an hour's ride from Albany, New York. Still as a mountain, it walked, talked, and smelled of the country.

When we were preparing to leave in August for the novitiate, Dad asked us if we really wanted to go there. We replied, "Yes, certainly." We felt loved by Dad; looking back, it must have been difficult for him to let two of his sons leave home at the same time. His question also made us realize that we had a choice to enter God's service or not. Until that point we had never really questioned our decision to become friars.

What impelled us to go to the novitiate? We were very idealistic and wanted to make a difference in the world, but really entered the novitiate to seek after the kingdom of God, in accordance with the words in Matthew's Gospel "What shall it profit a person to gain the whole world and suffer the loss of his immortal soul?" We gave up family, dating, possessions— everything worldly—in order to gain purity of heart. We guided our lives with reference to purity of heart like a carpenter's rule. As friars we still had worldly thoughts. It's as impossible to stop the mind as it is to stop a windmill from turning. As the Hindu proverb puts it, "The human mind is like a monkey stung by a scorpion and drunk with alcohol." No sooner does one drive one thought out of one's mind then another thought enters. We soon found out that the Hindu proverb made a lot of sense for those who tried meditation for the first time.

DONNING THE HABIT

The novitiate year began with a formal ceremony in the chapel. Each postulant received the black tunic and white cord with the three knots symbolizing the vows of poverty, chastity, and obedience. To become a friar meant to cross a real frontier. We thought it appropriate to have distinctive clothing. It let everyone know that we professed a godly life. Those who met us expected appropriate behavior.

By donning the habit we were inserted into a venerable and ancient tradition dating back not only to the time of St. Francis in the twelfth century but dating back to the Longer Rule of St. Basil. St. Basil noted that this profession by means of clothing forms a kind of discipline for the weaker brethren. In this way they are kept from evil deeds even against their will. To have a distinctive dress implied that one had to live up to the profession that the clothing signified. Weaker friars would be helped to live a religious or pious life, even against their will. Our new clothing symbolized our separation from the world. By becoming Franciscan friars we twins were irrevocably separated from the world of the less committed. Internally, the separation from the world and our family and friends proved to be painful.

In fact, the isolation and solitude of the novitiate year got to us. We had known something of what to expect from friends who went through the novitiate. They warned us that if we were told to plant a tree or flower upside down we should do so without questioning the order. The trial of obedience has always been a general rule for admission to a religious order. Sulpicius Severus (360–420 C.E.), historian and hagiographer, related that one abbot in Egypt commanded a postulant to throw himself into a blazing oven. Another monk sent a candidate to water a stick in the earth, treating it as if it were an actual living plant. The oven apparently extinguished itself immediately so that the postulant did not receive burns and the stick actually bloomed at the end of a three-year period. We tried to be prepared for what might be asked of us.

At the novitiate we had to shed our previous names. Every friar in the Province of the Immaculate Conception had to choose a new name and most of the common names were already taken. Since we were twins, our classmates suggested names for us like Hit and Miss, Prosit and Deo Gratias (the traditional Latin terms used in the refectory giving the friars permission to talk during meals), or Zig and Zag. We also had to take Mary as our middle name 'Mary' in honor of the mother of Jesus. Bobby chose to be called Allen, while Richie assumed the name of Linus.

ON COUNTRY LIVING

During the year of novitiate we spent our time in prayer, meditation, reciting the breviary, classroom work, doing chores, and camaraderie. The year started off with a ten-day retreat during which time we were not allowed to speak at all. This proved to be a struggle for us since we were extroverts by nature. Intellectually, we thought of silence as the point in life's hourglass through which our patience had to be tested. Emotionally, we found it difficult to adjust to a rural environment since we had hitherto lived only in the hustle and bustle of the city.

Time seemed to stand still as we worked in the fields planting potatoes and vegetables and later in the kitchen canning food. Our days fell like rain drops in the surge of the sea. In the novitiate we were close to nature which made us think of God. We were reminded of Charles Hanon Towne's words, "Thrice eloquent are quiet trees . . . yet how they speak of God."

We had difficulty adjusting to country living. For example, when the several pigs and piglets bolted from their pens, we helped round them up. Both of us were a bit nervous to wrestle a hog to the ground so we "made believe" we were trying to grasp one but never really tried that hard, hoping that someone else would do the job.

Class work offered little challenge. We had to translate the Constitution of the Conventual Franciscans from Latin into English. We also studied the Rule of St. Francis and ascetical theology, which though important did not tax our brains. Intellectually speaking, Linus became upset when Father Celestine Regnier, the Novice Master, confiscated his copy of Aristotle's *Opera Omnia*. The novitiate housed a small library containing books on piety and prayer such as St. Thomas a Kempis' *Introduction to the Devout Life*, but nothing that stimulated us intellectually.

In the minor seminary we had a lot of joy in our lives. There the friars in charge believed in the axiom *mens sana in corpore sano*, or a "sound mind, in a sound body." In the novitiate that rule did not hold. A ton of manual work did not sit well with us and we sorely missed organized recreational activities. We felt that we were constantly under the surveillance of the Novice Master, Father Celestine, who came across more like a drillmaster in the Marines than a compassionate friar. He loved to put on plays, but drama did not appeal to us. Richie wrote an article for a popular Franciscan magazine, *The Companion of St. Francis and St. Anthony*. Instead of encouraging Richie for his effort, Father Celestine subjected the piece to a severe critique. Father Declan, the Novice Master's assistant, surprised us by his kind and easy-going nature. Overall, the atmosphere in the novitiate might be best summed up by the words, fearful and oppressive.

Upon reflection, it's amazing that we did not throw in the towel. Because we looked at the novitiate as a kind of boot camp that had to be endured in order to move on to the next phase of our lives—the major seminary where we would study philosophy and theology—the thought of a bright and hopeful future kept us going.

During the novitiate year Linus became very scrupulous. One who has a scrupulous conscience is like the person who has an annoying pebble in his/her shoe that constantly acts as an irritant. At one point he went to confession three times a week and still felt estranged from God. On an overcast day the sun still shines brightly, but one doesn't feel its rays since they are hidden by the clouds. Both of us wanted to somehow feel God's loving presence, but God appeared to us like that sun on a cloudy day, that is, hidden behind the clouds.

ANYONE CARE FOR TOAST?

In the spring many of the novices became very sick with a stubborn stomach virus. Our family doctor put the blame on an onion patch running through our well water. It took three weeks of terrible discomfort before we recovered.

In the novitiate, we were known for our huge appetites. One day before Lent Father Celestine told the class that he had observed two of the friars chow down 36 slices of toast between them at breakfast. Bobby downed 19 slices, Richie a mere 17. He did not mention any names. However, after class he took us aside and we steeled ourselves for the punishment we expected to receive. Instead, we were dumbfounded when he said that we obviously had a metabolic problem and that he would excuse us from the upcoming Lenten fast. Needless to say, sheer joy impelled us to jump about two feet off the ground.

During Fridays in Lent we were instructed to practice self-flagellation. In the privacy of our rooms we were to strip to our waist at the sound of the bell. Then we were to hit ourselves with the cord around our waists that had three knots symbolizing the three vows of poverty, chastity, and obedience. We were to do this in imitation of the sufferings of Christ. The exercise lasted about ten minutes. We heard loud noises from the friar whose room was adjacent to ours. Afterwards, we asked him why all that commotion. He explained that he considered the entire exercise to be crazy so he spent his time beating his bed, claiming "it was easier on his back."

The novitiate lasted one entire year and one day. We never understood the significance of that one day. At the end of that year we made a ten-day silent retreat and then pronounced our simple vows. They were called simple because they were only good for three years. After three years we would make our solemn vows which lasted a lifetime. We then went back to St. Anthony on Hudson in Rensselaer, New York, for the summer before heading off to complete our college education in Granby, Massachusetts.

ST. ANTHONY ON HUDSON

Rensselaer, New York, separated from Albany by the Hudson River, served as the location of the major seminary of the Conventual Franciscans of the Immaculate Conception Province. St. Anthony's, situated on Van Rensselaer's former estate, boasted a sprawling green lawn that led up to the Manor House. The Manor House had an old but stately structure with ceilings about fifteen feet high and a fireplace in every room.

As young friars we were thrilled to spend the summer at St. Anthony's on the Hudson. The Cleric Master, Father Hugh De Cicco, a well-intentioned person tended to be very rigid. We watched movies and munched on pizza on Saturday nights. On occasion some of the friars might drive up to Saratoga to take in an outdoor concert with the group, Chicago, or drive to Tanglewood, Massachusetts, to hear the Boston Pops Symphony Orchestra.

We also received three weeks' vacation at Raquette Lake, New York, in the heart of the Adirondack State Park. One needed a boat to access the summer camp owned by the Franciscans. Nestled in the woods, it had its own bright chapel. We were warned to be aware of brown bears, particularly mothers with cubs. The weather could be damp and rainy. One time it rained almost every day for two weeks straight. Still, one could play pinochle or chess and read. When the weather turned ugly, we often read a book a day. On sunny days one could go swimming and fishing or take an all-day canoe trip. Both of us loved to swim and fish.

The camp also had a sailboat, in fact, a lightning because it went really fast in a stiff wind. One day we were two of nine friars on board when we capsized. Richie, sunning himself on the bow of the sailboat hit the water fast and got tangled in the sails. Three of the friars were non-swimmers but miraculously clutched the side of the boat after it was righted. Bob uttered a sigh of relief after Richie miraculously surfaced after being caught in the sails. Both of us were thankful to be alive and well.

We both loved to spend an hour a day in meditation at the chapel located on the campgrounds. Our prayer at this point progressed from discursive prayer to the next level, the illuminative stage. That is to say, we did not so much think when we prayed but let God come and flood us with her grace. This occurred on a regular basis. The grace of God completely filled our inner being so that we were transported, as it were, beyond space and time into a no-thinking, all-receiving zone. All we had to do in prayer is be open to God's grace, and then the Hound of Heaven took over, to do what God wanted to do in terms of touching our inner being.

One summer, though, the Provincial (equivalent to the C.E.O. of a company), Father William D'Arcy, noticed how thin we looked. At that time we weighed about 125 pounds soaking wet, and he told us that we could spend six weeks at Raquette Lake instead of the normal three. We jumped for joy at his largesse, although some of the friars felt we were getting preferential treatment.

BEHIND THE KIELBASA CURTAIN

The summer ended almost as soon as it began, and we found ourselves in the Franciscan college of St. Hyacinth in Granby, Massachusetts run by the friars of the Polish Province. We found the discipline tough, the studies intense, and the food terrible. Granby had a different feel to it than did the friaries run by the friars of the German province, Immaculate Conception. One of our friars quipped that it felt we were behind the Kielbasa Curtain.

At Granby the Polish superiors put more emphasis on manual labor and less time on sports. Our Cleric Master, Father Ferdinand Cisek, though outwardly intense had, in fact, an easygoing temperament. We brought with us to Granby some of our own friars to teach, namely, Father Bruce Ritter, the Assistant Cleric Master, who taught American literature; Father Reynold Kowalski, whom we knew well from the minor seminary, who taught English literature; Father Owen Bennett, a philosopher; and Father Venance Harkness, a psychologist. The friars from St. Anthony Province had to study Polish, a difficult language to learn for those who did not speak it at home before joining the Franciscans.

FATHER ADAM

The rector and president of the college, Father Adam Zajdel, taught us sociology. Actually, we taught sociology to ourselves for the most part. He would spend class time reading the book to us or having us answer the questions in the book at the end of the chapter. By teaching this course himself, Father Adam saved the college money. However, our education suffered.

Father Adam rarely smiled, which added to his hard exterior. He drove a tractor and had boundless energy for working in the field. All generally feared him. One day while leading meditation in chapel, one of the brother candidates, who was rather rotund, fell asleep in the pew. We then heard a loud thud, indicating that he had actually fallen while asleep into the middle aisle of the chapel floor. So as not to incur the wrath of Father Adam, the candidate pretended that he fainted but we all knew otherwise. At breakfast we had a hearty laugh over this incident.

LIFE AS A TWIN

Our rooms at St. Hyacinth College were located right next to each other on the second floor. The rooms were large and attractive with soft wooden floors. The chapel, the library, the classrooms, and our living quarters were housed in one enormously large building. We only had one serious disagreement with each other during our two-year stay in Granby. We can't remember what caused it. It led to a fight in which Richie hit Bobby in the face with a punch. Bobby was really hurt by the punch, and Richie cried knowing that he hit him harder than he intended.

We were both upset when one of the Polish friars, Friar Bartholomew, developed leukemia and died at 19 years of age. Bart's death, reminded us of our own mortality and the Polish friars who knew and loved him, grieved for weeks on end as did his family. He went so fast that his death hardly seemed possible, but we were not led to question God's existence nor did it hinder our prayer life. We found support during these days in prayer.

During our two-year stint in Granby we got to admire the Polish friars, especially their work ethic. Compared to them the friars of the German province were soft. They worked hard in the fields and in the classroom, where they also excelled, and on Saturday night some of them enjoyed playing the accordion and dancing the Polka. We called one of their favorite tunes "Ice Cubes and Beer."

At Granby grades were over-emphasized. At the end of the semester they were posted on the main bulletin board on the main floor of the college so everyone could see how others fared. This bothered us tremendously, making us competitive with each other and with the other friars. Those in charge thought that this would motivate us to do well. Instead, it had the opposite effect and made us feel poorly about ourselves.

GRADUATION

We graduated from St. Hyacinth College in Granby on June 10th, 1963, a big day for us, not only because we were the first in our family to graduate from college. Dad and our other brothers drove to Granby on that day to rejoice with us. That added to the specialness of the day. We were happy to receive our B.A. degrees in Philosophy. The local bishop and the respective Provincials of the German (Immaculate Conception) and Polish (St. Anthony's) provinces handed us our diplomas.

The next chapter deals with a low moment in our lives as twins: separation from each other. Bobby pursued his studies in theology at St. Anthony on Hudson; Richie meanwhile studied in Innsbruck, Austria. The separation felt like death.

COUNTING OUR BLESSINGS

1. Our time with the Franciscans helped us discover our intellectual vocation. We learned that we would never make a mark in the world by working with our hands in a craft or trade, as did many of our relatives. Rather, we would nurture others through counseling, as in the case of Bobby, who went into psychotherapy, or by helping them grow intellectually, as in the case of Richie, who would become a university professor.
2. The seminary taught us that our lives would develop like trees spreading deep roots among our peers, while simultaneously coming closer to God through prayer. Our growth would be both vertical and horizontal at the same time.
3. We gained a sense of mastery in the Franciscans. We arrived uncertain and unsure of ourselves. We emerged with a strong faith in God, compassion for others, particularly for the poor, and a sense of optimism concerning the future.

Richie on the left. Bobby on the right. Frank, our older brother, in the middle.

Our paternal grandparents, John and Anna Penaskovic.

Our maternal grandparents, Elvira, on the left, Vincent, Mom's stepfather, on the right. The children, Jean, our Mom as a child, her step-brother, Ted, and her step-sister, Marie.

Our aunt, Helen Lipinski, on the left, Grandma Anna on the right.

Dora Bolger and Joe Bolger on their wedding day.

Graduation from St. Joe's grammar school. Bob on the extreme left; Richie on the extreme right.

Joe Bolger on the left, Richie on the right. Cousin Dora seated.

Bill, our brother, kneeling on the left. Bob on the left, Dad next to Bob, Frank in the middle. Richie standing on the right next to Tom, kneeling.

Richie on the left. Bobby on the right.

Chapter Four

A Fork in the Road

"Companionship with the good is like walking through dew and mist; although they do not drench your clothing, in time it becomes imbued with moisture."

Guishan, a Zen Master

"Joys and sorrows are time-born and cannot last.
Therefore, do not be perturbed by these.
The greater the difficulties and obstructions,
The more intense will be your endeavor to cling to His feet
And the more will your prayer increase from within.
And when the time is ripe,
You will gain mastery over this power."

Sri Anandamayi Ma

The skin is not the only boundary around the self. Other people are a real part of us and when we are separated from them, the pain can be acute. We experienced a jarring loss when we were twenty-two years old. Bobby Brown took his theological studies in the United States at St. Anthony on Hudson, the major seminary of the Conventual Franciscan friars of the Immaculate Conception Province. His twin, Richie Blue, meanwhile, would be sent to study theology in Innsbruck, Austria. The separation would unleash a huge amount of emotional and psychic pain.

We will let Bobby tell his story in his own words. Then, Richie will get his chance to describe his four-year stay in Austria and Germany.

BOBBY BROWN AT RENSSELAER, NEW YORK

After graduating from St. Hyacinth College in Granby, Massachusetts in 1963, I began my theological studies at St. Anthony's major seminary, situated across the Hudson River from Albany, New York. On my first visit to St. Anthony's, the beauty of the large stately trees shaking in the breeze struck me, and my eyes were riveted on the carefully mowed lawns that stretched out interminably.

The seminary consisted of a Manor House built around 1839 by the architect and engineer, Frederick Diaper in the architectural style known as Greek revival. It originally housed William van Rensselaer and others and became known as Beverwyck House, since centuries ago, the Dutch used the word, Beverwyck, for Albany.

The Manor House, formerly known as Beverwyck, may be found in the National Register of Historical Homes for two reasons: its age and its marble staircase. These stairs are considered an architectural masterpiece since they have no support on one entire side, yet were fashioned entirely out of heavy marble. The building has huge rooms with a fireplace in each room and 12–15 foot ceilings. Even today the Manor House stands proud and noble, a unique and impressive structure. Besides the Manor House, St. Anthony's had an adjoining clericate for the friars, a large and spacious gym, built by the friars themselves, a sister's convent, an apiary, printing shop, bookbinding facility, library, music room, and a large garage. One could learn a trade or develop one's talents in such areas as music, library science, or printing.

Since three of our classmates were sent abroad to study, Friar Dominic Mc Gee and I were the only first-year theology students at St. Anthony on Hudson. After separating from Richie, I became sick the first year at Rensselaer with a stomach problem. I felt lost and disoriented without the emotional support of my twin. Medication helped a bit and I began counseling with our moral theology professor, Father Berard Reigert, a clinical psychologist.

My superior at St. Anthony's kept me very busy. In addition to my theological studies, I helped the procurator with the finances, such as paying bills. I drove a tractor to mow the vast lawn and drove into Albany each week to collect used stamps from the Department of Motor Vehicles and other locations. St. Anthony's possessed twin 35-millimeter motion picture cameras. We viewed first-run films without interruption, projected on a large screen. We saw foreign films and had one of the friars research the film ahead of time. He would then lead a discussion of the films by such well-known directors as Federico Fellini and Ingmar Bergman.

On weekends I accompanied the Chaplain, Father Fidelis, to the Albany County Jail and to the Ann Lee Home for the elderly to celebrate Mass and interact with the laity. Measured by any yardstick Father Fidelis completely smashed the mold of a typical friar. He had very definite views about life and frequently espoused right-wing political views. He preached passionately, even vociferously yet was an extremely kind friar. As a result of my experience at the jail, I became interested in the plight of prisoners. Perhaps that's the reason why my first job in civilian life involved working with the Nassau County Probation Department.

Aside from the fact that I missed my twin so very much, I generally enjoyed life at St. Anthony on Hudson. We had a marvelous group of friars who were very supportive of each other. We prayed hard, studied hard, and laughed a lot. There was a fantastic spirit of cooperation and brotherly love among the friars and staff. Father Aidan Carr taught us canon law and we greatly appreciated the fact we could approach him with any problem. A deeply spiritual person Fr. Aidan became the editor of a nationally known journal for priests called *The Homiletic and Pastoral Review*. Later on, he would leave the Franciscans and join the Trappist monastery at Mempkin Corners in North Carolina. In time his fellow monks elected him their Abbot. A wise choice indeed.

Father Conan Lynch, our immediate superior, bore the honorific title, Cleric Master. He taught us biblical studies and Hebrew and often joined us in a basketball or baseball game. Father Peter Damian Fehlner taught us dogmatic theology and lived up to his reputation as the brightest person on the faculty, hands down. His expertise extended to the game of chess for which he had no match among any of the friars. Father Berard Reigert taught us moral theology and introduced us to Martin Luther King Jr. and the whole civil rights movement.

Life did not consist entirely of prayer and study. The Conventual Franciscans rolled up their sleeves to lend a helping hand to the poor in Albany. We conducted a revision of the housing codes in the downtrodden areas of the inner city that were being dismantled in order to make way for the new state office buildings soon to be erected. We worked together with a minority social worker at the Clinton Avenue Neighborhood Association to involve minority youths in after-school social and recreational programs.

We attended lectures from the head of the National Association for the Advancement of Colored Persons (NAACP), when he came to visit Albany. In the spirit of the Second Vatican Council, which ran from 1962–65, we also participated in interfaith dialogues with Jewish, Muslim, and Protestant clergy and laity in the spirit of the Second Vatican Council that ran from 1962–1965. These were the days when the ecumenical movement, the drive toward unity among the various churches and religious groups, had its heyday and we joined in the dialogue with our Protestant clergy and Jewish rabbis.

The latter told us the prejudice they encountered over the centuries and we listened compassionately to their tale.

After my two-year stint at St. Anthony on Hudson, the Immaculate Conception Province of the Conventual Franciscans decided to build a spanking new building to house the theology students complete with a modern chapel in the spirit of the Second Vatican Council. The altar, set squarely in the center of the chapel, became the focal point of the entire building. I loved watching the builders construct the new structure and I shared my excitement about the construction of this state-of-the-art facility in letters to Richie, who was living in Wuerzburg, Germany, at the time. The old clericate then became home to college students preparing for the priesthood. In addition to the novitiate at Middleburg, the friars established a second novitiate in Washington, D.C.

The Sixties were a time of rapid change in society at large with the Hippies and the Flower Children. The winds of change were strong and seemingly overnight shook the bastions of the Roman Catholic Church. This spirit of change filtered down to St. Anthony's. The friars tried hard to develop a renewed sense of community. St. Anthony's initiated a program in pastoral counseling, spearheaded by Father Jeffrey Keefe, a clinical psychologist. Father Jeffrey initiated studies in the psychodynamics of personality and I became a devotee of this newly-minted knowledge.

For our fifth year of theology my classmate, Friar Dominic and I, were assigned to a Franciscan parish for a year to do a practicum in pastoral studies. We tape-recorded our sessions of pastoral counseling and found Father Jeffrey's critique an excellent learning experience. We attended lectures on pastoral counseling and did an in-house residence at a drug rehabilitation center, Daytop Village, in Staten Island, New York. We also heard lectures on disabilities at Willowbrook, a state facility for severely retarded children in Staten Island.

I found contentment and peace of mind at St. Anthony's on Hudson. I thoroughly enjoyed the support I received from the community of friars. In retrospect I would give the pastoral internship very high marks. I also began individual psychotherapy with Father Jeffrey during the last two years of my theological education.

Some of the friars studying at St. Anthony's hailed from our missionary outposts in Costa Rica, Brazil, and the Far East. These friars brought an international dimension to St. Anthony's. They enriched our culture by introducing us to their world. We thoroughly enjoyed their food and their friendship. They taught us how to play their game, soccer.

During the Christmas and Easter holidays we friars had an opportunity to function as acolytes and deacons at some of the surrounding parishes. We heard lectures from missionaries and expanded our knowledge of some of the local customs in such far-flung areas as Africa, South America, particularly Brazil, and Latin America.

Summers were spent at a secluded spot in the Adirondack Mountains of upstate New York, Raquette Lake. The Franciscans set up a summer camp in a remote location, accessible only by water. Here we learned how to sail, water-ski, and launch a powerboat. The friars who went to summer school at the Catholic University of America in Washington, D.C. arrived for their vacation in August. Those friars who remained at St. Anthony on Hudson vacationed during June and July.

In my final year at St. Anthony on Hudson I became dean of students and had the responsibility to interact with the Cleric Master on behalf of the other students. I thoroughly enjoyed the freedom to run errands into Albany and the surrounding towns. I also had the opportunity to preach as a deacon and to officiate at funerals and weddings.

RICHIE AT INNSBRUCK AND WUERZBURG

My life might have turned out differently if I had been sent to Rome for my theological education rather than to the University of Innsbruck, Austria and the University of Wuerzburg, Germany. If I had spent nine years in the hothouse atmosphere of the Eternal City I might have become rigid in my theology and unable to leave the priesthood later on in life.

The theological training received in Rome at the Conventual Franciscan House of Studies located on Via San Teodoro, or at the Seraphicum, which was built later, could simply not compare with the theology taught at the University of Innsbruck. Josef Jungmann, one of the architects of the Constitution on the Liturgy adopted by the Second Vatican Council in 1963, taught liturgical studies at Innsbruck, as did Karl Rahner who taught dogmatic theology at Innsbruck from 1949–64. Both Jungmann and Rahner were named *periti* or theological advisors to the bishops assembled at the Second Vatican Council from 1962–65.

Rahner, arguably the greatest Catholic theologian in the twentieth century, wrote a score of books and articles, ranging from highly technical theological tomes to popular works on Ignatian spirituality. Much of Rahner's output took the form of articles. Many of his essays in theology were published in a multivolume work called *Theological Investigations*. The critical spirit of inquiry found among professors and students of theology in Innsbruck and Wuerzburg could not be duplicated in Rome.

Ever since the middle of the nineteenth century, Roman theology lost its edge remaining conservative, stodgy, and scholastic. Scholasticism, a method of scholarly inquiry, functioned originally as a teaching device in the universities of Western Europe from the end of the 11th to the 16th centuries, when it came under severe attack from humanist scholars, who stressed a more historical and literary approach to ancient literature.

After the 16th century scholasticism became restricted to philosophy and theology, and by the nineteenth century the Roman Catholic Church used the scholastic method exclusively. Students studying for the priesthood from the middle of the nineteenth century to the start of the Second Vatican Council in 1962 studied scholasticism. The Scholastic textbooks, written in Latin, consisted of theses and arguments drawn from scripture and tradition to support these theses. Critics would describe it as a cookie cutter approach to theology with an almost complete disregard for history and the historical context.

Students were expected to memorize the arguments verbatim. The scholastic method left little room for creativity either on the part of the professors or the students. The method did not encourage critical thinking. Students were, for the most part, put into a passive, acquiescent mode. There were some notable exceptions such as Bernard Lonergan's classes in dogmatic theology at the Gregorian University in Rome, and Bernard Haring's lectures on moral theology at the Academia Alfonsianum in the Eternal City.

In the nineteenth century the Roman Catholic Church favored the centralization of authority and influence in the Pope and in the Curia, as opposed to national or diocesan independence. This tendency became known as Ultramontanism. A famous Ultramontanist, William George Ward (1812–1882), upheld papal infallibility and aggressively pushed his anti-liberal views. He once quipped that he wished that the Pope would publish a new encyclical every day so that he could read it along with his morning newspaper.

Ultramontanism became more powerful as national and centrifugal movements such as Gallicanism and Josephinism became discredited, either because they lent countenance to the new liberal, anti-Christian movements of which the French Revolution was the most logical expression, or because they were heretical. The Ultramontanists forcefully opposed the rising theological liberalism of the day.

Geographically, the distance between Rome and Innsbruck amounted to a 17-hour train ride. Intellectually, the two cities remained light years away. The Austrian and German theologians had a tradition, going back to Vatican I in 1870, of standing up to Rome and thinking for themselves. I am thinking of the likes of Ignaz von Doellinger who rejected the definition of infallibility at Vatican I and of Herman Schell, professor of fundamental theology at Wuerzburg. Schell had two of his works placed on the Index of Forbidden Books by Rome in 1898.

Seminarians who studied scholasticism in Rome often emerged from the experience with tunnel vision and a fierce emotional attachment to the Holy See so that they never questioned papal teaching. In fact, that's the reason why many U.S. bishops sent the best and the brightest seminarians to Rome for their theological training. However, there was more prestige attached to studying at Innsbruck rather than at Rome with the possible exception of the Gregorianum or the Biblicum. The Germans had a saying that a Roman doctor of theology was equivalent to a German jackass. I do not agree with that particular perception but it is telling.

In Innsbruck we received a blow-by-blow account of the events of the Second Vatican Council daily at lunch and clapped thunderously when the Constitution on the Liturgy passed muster at the Council. We followed closely every move of that heady council. More importantly, I might not have been able to leave the priesthood if I had not been introduced to the forward-thinking mindset of the seminarians at the Canisianum in Innsbruck who challenged my theological assumptions every step of the way, particularly in regard to the use of contraceptives for married couples. I found it difficult, at first, to accept the arguments of my peers at Innsbruck that artificial contraception may be morally correct for married couples. Over time I came to see that in today's world artificial contraception might be a necessity, particularly in poor countries.

At Innsbruck I thrilled to hear Josef Jungmann, a peritus at the Council, lecture on the liturgy. I also had several conversations with Hugo Rahner, S.J. a well-known patristic scholar, teacher extraordinaire, and the brother of Karl Rahner, one of the most distinguished theologians of the 20th century. The Americans at the Canisianum, (affectionately called "the Can"), kidded Hugo about translating his brother Karl's works "into German" because Karl's high-sounding German bore the marks of a very dense philosopher, Martin Heidegger. The average German cannot understand Heidegger's opaque prose, in part, because he coined German words as he went along.

The Americans at the Can numbered about 50, some of whom appeared to me at the time as having graduated from culinary school because they simply excelled as cooks. The food served at the Can left everything to be desired unless one liked tripe, and considered tongue a delicacy. In regard to eating tongue, I once stated, "I did not care to eat something that was in someone else's mouth." I also could not stand the skim milk that was boiled and served at breakfast. The smell alone almost knocked me over. All of the veterans, particularly the American contingent, at the Can had hot plates in which they cooked their own food and invited friends over for supper. They tried to outdo each other as chefs, much to my palate's delight.

Seminarians from other countries at the Can, particularly those from Switzerland, Germany and other parts of Austria, studied in Innsbruck as much for the opportunity to go skiing during the fall semester as to do serious theology. Groupings or cliques were formed along nationalistic lines, each nation trying to outdo the others, much like an Olympian meet, except this particular Olympiad lasted 365 days a year.

Our ship set sail on the S.S. Atlantic commanded by Capt. Charles Reilly on a Vagabond Cruise to the Mediterranean departing from New York harbor at noon on September 18, 1963. Our party consisted of our leader, Father Peter Damian Fehlner, Father David Hammond who was returning to Rome to work toward his doctorate in canon law, Friar Patrick Gallagher, who would study in Rome along with our classmate, Ernest Ruede, and John Burkhard who would be studying with me in Innsbruck.

A few days before our departure for Europe our confreres at the major seminary of the Conventual Franciscans in Rensselaer, New York feted us to a farewell party, which included five skits. We also enjoyed a farewell party in our stateroom dockside three hours before departure. Many of the friars attended, including our Minister Provincial, Father David Schultz. The saddest farewell involved my twin brother, Bob. My heart ached when I hugged him goodbye. The impact of our separation did not hit me straightaway because I was at first taken with the excitement of the trip. But then it hit me like a sledgehammer and I was clobbered. More about that later.

I enjoyed cruising on the North Atlantic Ocean and one day I spotted a sailfish running alongside the ship, much to my delight. As an extrovert I make friends easily, striking up an acquaintance with two co-eds from Villanova who were going to a tour of Italy. They had trouble as we disembarked the ship in Naples and asked me to help but my superior, Father Peter Damian, told me not to help them. Why, I'm not sure of even until this day, but I felt badly at the time that I could not rescue those two damsels in distress. Perhaps that event should have made me question my commitment to the Franciscan Order, but it did not. A belly dancer provided entertainment on board the ship (that I would have liked to see just out of curiosity), but Father Peter Damian strictly forbade us to take in this particular show, much to my disappointment.

We passed the Azures during the night of September 24th and arrived in Lisbon, Portugal on the morning of September 26th. A large statue of Christ appeared in the distance as we cruised into the harbor. What a comforting sight, perhaps a sign of God's protection. For $25.00 we hired a taxi for the day to take us to see the sights. We visited gorgeous beaches such as Sintra and Estoril surrounding Lisbon, and noticed the Moorish influence on buildings in Lisbon and the surrounding area, dating back to 1147 when the Moors conquered this area. We also saw innumerable fish for sale on the docks where we anchored, and visited the church of St. Anthony of Lisbon, known by the Italians as St. Anthony of Padua.

On our brief stay in Tangiers, a city in Morocco, I remember vividly how ten Muslims in traditional dress were taking a nap in the street at mid-day. No sooner did we disembark then an enterprising Arab volunteered to take us to the Kasbah. Born and raised in the New York metropolitan area, I am naturally suspicious of strangers and told the man, "No dice."

From Tangiers we headed for Naples where the friars from *Bella Napoli* met us at the ship and took us to the friary in a poor section of town. We could see Mt. Etna in the distance and I tipped my hat to her imposing natural beauty.

The friars took us to the black market in beautiful Naples where one could purchase American cigarettes, guns, knives, wallets- all at bargain prices because most of the items for sale were so "hot" (stolen) that one needed gloves to handle them. I remember the crowd of people there. The Neapolitans had a reputation for thievery, one well deserved, judging from the sheer size of the market. We were told never to drive a car with foreign plates to Naples, particularly if one valued the contents left in the back seat, the trunk, or even the car itself for that matter. We also viewed the statue of St. Januarius, bishop and martyr. A vial containing the blood of St. Januarius becomes liquefied every year for the last 400 years. The liquefaction of the Saint's blood occurs on September 19th, his feast day, much to the amazement of the Neapolitan faithful.

From Naples we took the train to Rome. We stood for the five-hour ride. I fell asleep standing up in the aisle, held securely in place by the sheer size of the crowd. Rome completely took my breath away. It's the kind of city that one can see something new every single day of the year such as St. Peter's Basilica, the Coliseum, the catacombs of St. Callistus on the Appian Way, and the Vatican Library. Italian drivers scared me. Crossing the street on the zebra stripes for pedestrians amounted to a do-or-die situation. In Rome I first tasted the exquisiteness of Chianti, the sparkling flavor of Lambrusco and the sweetness of Italian port wine.

The Italian friars we met struck us as warm and gracious. Although conservative in their theology, they possessed a terrific sense of humor and had a knack for making visitors feel at home. They lived on a street called San Teodoro, where the residents knew enough not to dig for fear of finding an underground treasure. If this happened the Italian government claimed the property for itself as a national treasure.

Father Peter Damian put us on a train headed straight up the Alps to Innsbruck, our destination. En route to Innsbruck my stomach felt really bad after eating some apples of all things. I arrived at the Innsbruck train station with terrible heartburn and feeling quite punky. My German at the time left everything to be desired. The Franciscans had sent us to Innsbruck but did not give us a German language course to prepare us for study at a German-speaking university. This put a lot of pressure on us.

I never felt quite at home at Innsbruck. I had great difficulty adjusting to the mountain climate. After visiting Innsbruck in later life I still do not feel comfortable in Innsbruck. Part of the problem involved a wind called the *Foehn*. It comes from the south in winter and hangs around the mountains for a few days. Many natives of Innsbruck are also bothered by this wind, developing headaches and stomach aches. These are the symptoms that I developed. The police in Innsbruck say that there are more traffic accidents during the time of the *Foehn* than at any other time of the year.

The Canisianum seemed cold and dreary. The other Americans were a terrific group, but I missed the closeness of the Franciscan community of friars. One of the seminarians from the Buffalo diocese liked to eat out. Each time he would carefully read the menu, ask the waitress about particular items on the menu, only at the end to invariably order beef tartar. I especially liked Jay Davidson who matriculated us at the University because of our ignorance of the German language. I found it difficult to relate to the superior of the Canisianum, a Jesuit priest called Pater Regens or Father in Charge. I remember him as a serious person with a quick wit and no-nonsense personality.

The deeper reason why I felt out of sorts at Innsbruck had to do with the fact that I sorely missed my twin brother, Bob, although I didn't realize this at the time. I depended on Bob to make my tie and read my mind. I always had my twin brother at my side and had taken his presence for granted. Now left on my own, I could not depend on his guidance and help in time of troubled water. Depressed by my situation, I went to an Austrian psychiatrist who prescribed a drug called Belladonna. I hated taking the medication because it made me feel sluggish.

My life was definitely at ebb tide. I often had stomach pains and headaches. Remarkably, my twin developed the same symptoms himself, although I never told him or anyone else of my condition. His symptoms mimicked mine. And he underwent the same kind of depression I experienced in Innsbruck. How did this come about? How did my twin know what I had been going through? Perhaps this might be called intuitive or extraordinary knowledge, the kind Elizabeth Lloyd Mayer speaks about in her book, *Extraordinary Knowing: Science, Skepticism, And The Inexplicable Powers Of The Human Mind.*

There's another reason why this proved to be a very trying time in my life. Our Franciscan superior, Father David Schultz, had sent us to Innsbruck without giving us a course in the German language. I matriculated as a first year student in theology at the University of Innsbruck in which the language of instruction was German and I lacked even a basic course in German.

In class I could only write down sounds, then ask a German-speaking student what German words these sounds represented. I then looked up their meaning in the German-English dictionary. This could not possibly be the best way to learn a foreign language. I once went to the grocery store and asked the owner if he could make me a ham sandwich. My German was so deficient that I ordered 6 kilos of ham, which came to roughly 15 pounds of meat, asking the owner if that was enough ham for a sandwich. He laughed heartily over this.

There were other memorable moments at Innsbruck. I took in a Western movie to improve my German. It tickled my funny bone to hear an American Indian say "Wie geht's" for "How." I laughed inappropriately in the Austrian movie theater, much to the chagrin of those seated near me.

In the course of the first semester, we did, however, have the benefit of having a basic introductory class in German taught by one of the students in the Can, Harry Eder. Harry had a Ph.D. in German and had a complete command of the language. Despite this class it takes more than a few weeks time to learn a language as difficult as German in order to take classes and pass examinations in a foreign language.

At the end of the first semester in Innsbruck my measly knowledge of German did not allow me to take oral exams. Fortunately, my professors at Innsbruck realized this and allowed many of us to take our exams in Latin. I had studied Latin for seven years and could take exams in Latin quite easily.

I remember the shock that came over me upon hearing the announcement in November of 1963 that our President, John F. Kennedy had been shot in Dallas. A few minutes later the radio announcer gave an update stating that Pres. Kennedy had indeed died. Boing. It seemed so eerie and unreal. I prayed for him and his family. The Europeans were also very upset with the news. When I traveled to Yugoslavia about a year later, the newspapers were loaded with stories about President Kennedy. The Europeans certainly loved J.F.K.

A key event occurred during December of 1963. John Burkhard and I received permission to travel to Wuerzburg, Germany and spend Christmas vacation with the Conventual Franciscan friars there. We had a wonderful time. The student friars were a diverse group. One hailed from Vienna, viz., Friar Albert, a stout friar enamored of canon law; two were from Belgium, one from Bordeaux, France; the rest were from different parts of Germany, Cologne, Mannheim, etc. They enjoyed telling us German jokes, which we didn't quite understand, and having us repeat them back with a thick American accent. While in Wuerzburg my health improved 100%. No more headaches and stomach pains from the *Foehn*. No colds, even though in the Franziskaner church at Wuerzburg the holy water in the font turned to ice on many a wintry day.

A warm spirit pervaded the friary at Wuerzburg. The Germans would call this spirit, *Gemuetlichkeit*, a word difficult to translate. It means a feeling of warmth, intimacy, and hospitality. Breakfast at the friary could be taken in the common room. One could choose from a wide assortment of cold cuts called *Wurst*. The friars laughed a lot and the superior, Father Walter Hof, may best be described as a kind, and soft-spoken man of about 50. I don't believe I ever heard him raise his voice.

The common room also contained copies of current periodicals dealing with theology and spirituality. Adjacent to the common room a small, theological library contained about a thousand books, which I devoured. When reading in that room I felt like I died and went to heaven.

I found it difficult to say goodbye to the friars at Wuerzburg and take the train back to Innsbruck. No sooner did I return to Innsbruck than my stomach pains commenced. I decided to write my superior, Father David Schulze, in Syracuse, New York asking permission to transfer to Wuerzburg for health reasons. Much to my delight permission came in two weeks time and I rejoiced. I would finish my semester at Innsbruck and then leave for Wuerzburg at the end of February. I informed the Jesuit, Father Regens, of this fact but he did not believe I really needed to transfer to Wuerzburg. Naturally, I would miss my confrere, John Burkhard, but my health would improve dramatically once I arrived in Wuerzburg.

As the only native speaker of English in the friary at Wuerzburg, necessity forced me to speak German the entire day. I also had a private tutor in the person of Friar Stephen Boymann from Cologne, an extremely kind, highly spiritual person, and a patient teacher as well.

The theology offered at the University of Wuerzburg had more in common with the Second Vatican Council than the theology I studied at Innsbruck. First, I noticed the strong biblical thrust at Wuerzburg, abetted by the scholarly work of Josef Zeigler and Rudolf Schnackenburg. I studied scripture nine hours a week. Joseph Ziegler taught me Old Testament and he went right from the Hebrew text. For the course on *Genesis* he would read the text in Hebrew, then recite the Septuagint text in Greek, and then give the Vulgate text in Latin. For good measure he would throw in the Arabic equivalents for some of the more important Hebrew words in *Genesis*.

Ziegler had to be the most learned man I knew, his memory, prodigious; his sense of humor, rare. He loved to regale his 200 students with stories and jokes. He could be a tough taskmaster. At a German university there were no term papers or mid-tem exams. One's grade depended entirely on a 10–15 minute oral exam given at the end of the semester.

For the oral exam he made students read the Hebrew text rapidly and then give the German translation. I found this to be a bit intimidating. Moreover, one could not easily pull the wool over Ziegler's eyes. He edited several important books of the Old Testament for the critical edition of the Septuagint Bible and knew his field backwards and forwards. I think I passed his course, in part, because, he took pity on foreign students.

Rudolf Schnackenburg had to be the second most learned man I knew. He did not have Ziegler's sense of humor, but students nevertheless flocked to his classes in droves. To take an oral exam with him proved to be an unforgettable experience, a real "treat." He asked me once how St. Paul in his epistles expresses our union with Christ. I muttered back an answer but not the one he wanted. I'll never forget his answer," St. Paul uses three ways to express our union with Christ, the "*suv*" prefix with certain Greek verbs, the "*ev Xristo*" formula and the possessive genitive." Wow. I could not believe that anyone could ask such minutiae on an exam and expect students to rattle back such trivial details.

One semester Schnackenburg accepted an invitation to be a distinguished visiting professor at Notre Dame. While there he took in a Notre Dame football game. In class he gave his German-speaking audience his take on college football. "These men line up against each other and then, after the referee blows a whistle, smash into one another, dragging each other to the ground. Sometimes they throw the ball a hundred feet downfield. They do this many times during the course of the game and then kick the football between two goalposts." As an American I found his version of college football quite amusing.

Second, one of the great advantages of studying in Wuerzburg had to be the opportunity to hear and see many of the brightest stars in the theological galaxy. I had the opportunity to hear Matthew Black from England discourse on textual criticism, Joachim Jeremias from Goettingen speak on the very words of Jesus, Josef Ratzinger, (better known today as Pope Benedict XVI) from Muenster wax eloquently on the collegiality of bishops, and Xavier Leon Dufour, S.J., from Lyons, France, give a scathing critique of Rudolf Bultmann. Karl Rahner from Munich, Walter Kasper from Tuebingen, Hans Urs von Balthasar from Einsiedeln, Switzerland, and Juergen Moltmann, who spoke on the theology of hope, were only some of the guest speakers at the University of Wuerzburg, I had the privilege to hear.

I had the opportunity to speak to the French philosopher Gabriel Marcel, the Jesuit theologian, Karl Rahner and the Swiss theologian, Hans Urs von Balthasar one on one. These experiences were unforgettable for me. Gabriel Marcel, an existentialist philosopher and French playwright, gave a talk to a standing room only audience in Wuerzburg on "Death and Immortality" in

1966. Marcel, one of the greatest living philosophers of the day, had some of his plays staged in Paris. After the talk I spoke to him for a while in German. He invited me to visit him in Paris. Regrettably, he passed away in 1968 before I could take him up on his offer.

I found Karl Rahner to be down to earth and approachable. Rahner, in particular, had a great sense of humor and did not take himself too seriously, as opposed to Hans Urs Von Balthasar who was more intense and serious. I told them of my work on John Henry Newman and both of them appeared interested in it. I also got to speak to Rahner some years later after a lecture in Munich, Germany. Rahner remains one of my heroes in theology and it warmed my heart to be able to converse with him one on one.

My knowledge of German became quite extensive because of my stay with the friars at Wuerzburg. Soon I found that I could read books and articles in theology without using a dictionary. Not only did I learn "high" German, but I also learned slang. I had to wear my Franciscan habit everywhere I went in town, including classes at the University. In the summer months the habit could be oppressive to wear, particularly on hot, humid days. On those days I wore my bathing suit underneath the habit.

Once a year the clerics or those studying for the priesthood were obligated to go out into the environs of Wuerzburg and beg for potatoes from the local farmers. I hated doing this for two reasons: I could not understand the farmers since they did not speak standard German but a local dialect called Franconian. In this dialect potatoes were called "Grumpi." In High German the word for potatoes was "Kartoffeln."

Also, I felt bad taking potatoes that I did not earn myself. I felt like a heel, taking advantage of peoples' generosity. We also had to stay overnight at a farmer's house and go from farm to farm pulling a large wagon on which the potatoes were placed. We then dragged the potato-laden wagon to a central location where a large truck from the friary would pick them up. We ate dinner with a German family. Those at dinner did not have their own drinking glass. Instead, a common cup circulated around the table from which everyone drunk. I found such a custom unsanitary and feared picking up a cold or something more serious such as the flu.

During days like these I missed my family. The pain came over me particularly during the Christmas season. Dad wrote to me faithfully every couple of weeks. Mom corresponded only occasionally and I dearly cherished her letters. My twin brother wrote to me often. I would remain in Germany four years without returning once to the U.S. I missed watching N.F.L. games on T.V. I totally immersed myself in my studies. I would spend several hours reading heavy theological tomes in the library on Christmas Day. I became very well versed in German theology.

Loneliness kept me company at Wuerzburg. I went for counseling to Dr. Wiesenhuetter whom I got to know as a professor. Wiesenhuetter and Heinz Fleckenstein, Professor of Pastoral Theology team-taught a seminar on pastoral counseling. Toward the end of the class they would break out a case of German beer, Wuerzburger Hofbraeu, and share it with the students. They would tell stories about such luminaries as Carl Jung, a famous Swiss psychiatrist, and Buitendijk, a well-known Dutch psychiatrist at the time.

Wiesenhuetter and I became good friends and disappointment weighed on my soul when he became professor of psychiatry in Tuebingen. Once matriculated in a German university, one could take courses in any department. I took a course in hypnosis from Dr. Wiesenhuetter. This course would serve me in good stead later on in life when for a brief period of time I became a hypnotist.

I also took graduate courses in philosophy at Wuerzburg. I attended an advanced seminar on Heidegger's famous book, *Being and Time*, one noted for its dense German. This forced me to read some sections of the book four or five times before I understood it. There were only five or six students in the class, which was run seminar style, truly a first-rate learning experience. We sat in a circle and took turns sharing our understanding of the text.

After two years in Wuerzburg I took a rigorous exam called the *Vorpruefung*. This exam, equivalent to the B.A. degree in theology, involved a two-hour written exam followed by an oral exam in Liturgy, Fundamental Theology, and Church History. I reveled in memorizing a plethora of material. Father Walter Hof, my German Master of Clerics, took great delight in the fact that I took this exam because many of the other friars, native speakers of German, refused to take these exams because they were demanding. He used me as an example to prod the other friars to sit for this examination.

In my fourth year I took what is called the *Hauptpruefung* or *Theol. Abschluss-Examen* in theology, equivalent to the M.A. in theology, the hardest exam I ever took. It involved writing a forty-page essay on a theological topic, and exams in six subjects: Introduction to the Bible, Old Testament Exegesis, New Testament Exegesis, Dogmatic Theology, Moral Theology, and Canon Law.

As the time for ordination drew near, I started to get cold feet. I really loved my studies and felt called by a divine Caller to be an academic. However, uncertainty came over me as I contemplated ordination to the priesthood. The very thought of my impending ordination frightened me. I felt like a feather carried hurriedly out to the deep by some very strong waves. I did not have much to say in the matter.

Little did I know at the time but similar thoughts raced through Bob's mind. He too experienced serious doubts about his upcoming ordination. He felt called to study psychotherapy more than work as an ordained priest for the rest of his life. I felt called to the intellectual life either as a professor or as a researcher in theology. In the end I consented to be ordained, saying to myself what other choice did I have? Once ordained, however, all my doubts vanished, at least for the first few years.

COUNTING OUR BLESSINGS

1. Although separated by 4,000 miles of ocean with loneliness, a constant companion, Bob and I became self-reliant. The pain of separation forced us to deepen our relationship with God. The pain of separation resembled broken bones. Yet broken bones when mended sometimes become stronger than the original ones. That's how it felt to us.
2. Suffering makes one compassionate. The deep pain we endured because of our separation made us more empathetic to those undergoing emotional turmoil, pain, and suffering. It enabled us to become better listeners to the people we would serve in our priestly ministry.
3. We found God's hand restorative and deeply healing, even when God wielded a scalpel. The cuts and wounds we received prepared us for our future work in the ministry. The friends and advisors who accompanied us on the way to ordination were God's saving ointment, which protected us from the wind and the cold. In sum, we were protected by God's soothing balm.
4. Living/traveling in Europe changed how we regarded the world. It made us view the U.S. through a different lens. Just as astronauts see planet Earth differently from the viewpoint of their spaceship, so too did we see the U.S. differently from across the Atlantic Ocean. We had much to be grateful for, such as indoor plumbing that our relatives in Yugoslavia did not have in the Sixties when Bob and I had visited them. We realized how much we had taken for granted life in the good old United States.

Chapter Five

Meeting the Pope

"The individual suffers because he perceives duality.
Find the One everywhere and in everything and
There will be an end to pain and suffering."

Sri Anandamayi Ma

"The day will come when, after harnessing the ether, the winds, the tides,
gravitation, we shall harness for God the energies of love. And, on that
day, for the second time in the history of the world, human beings will
have discovered fire."

Teilhard de Chardin

After her Swissair jet touched down in Switzerland, Cousin Helen Gala, who
had flown over for our ordination in Innsbruck, Austria, remarked that "the
airport personnel in Zurich spoke English with an accent," stating that "it was
hard to understand them." Her comments left me perplexed. I pointed out that
Switzerland was, indeed, a foreign country and that most of the population
spoke English only as a second language. "We should be glad that they speak
English at all," I added.

Ordination marked the culmination of twelve long years of study, discipline, and sacrifice, much like a cool breeze at the end of a long, hot, day.
Fittingly, on March 11, 1967 in Innsbruck, Austria, situated in the midst of
the Austrian Alps, Richie could see the majestic summit of Mt. Hafelkar,
(7,000 feet up on the Nordkette mountain range) from his window in the Canisianum. Bishop Paul Rausch of Innsbruck, Austria ordained us.

The day of ordination amounted to a shot of adrenaline, a supernatu-
ral high. Through the elaborate ritual of ordination, one became part of a

spiritual tradition stretching back to the priests, Melchisedch, Aaron, and Jesus himself. Ordination conferred privilege, responsibility, and a serious obligation to live up to the demands of the priestly office. It proved to be a decisive moment in our lives, one to be taken only after careful deliberation and discernment. We constituted a group of 25 new ordinandi. All of my American classmates at Innsbruck, including John Burkhard, were ordained with us twins.

Ordination changed one forever. One could now hear confessions, give absolution in the name of Christ, and change bread and wine into the body and blood of Jesus Christ, something not even the angels in heaven could do. As an ordained minister, people treated us differently. We were put on a pedestal and commanded immediate respect. No matter what one did, the faithful saw us as a representative of Christ himself. What a sobering thought.

We, twins, thrilled to be together after four long years of separation. Bobby Brown flew to Innsbruck along with Dad, our cousin, Helen Gala, and a friend, Cathy Burkhard. Bob described the trip to Innsbruck from Zurich on a small commuter plane as a harrowing experience. One had to fly between the Alps where there were strong air currents as the air hit the mountain tops, sending forth top winds. At one point the plane ride became so bumpy because of the high winds that the stewardess brought a drink to Bobby Brown on her hands and knees. Forty years ago a stewardess would do such things routinely. Today, the captain would have suspended in-flight service because of such turbulence.

We were overjoyed that some of our relatives and friends would be able to attend our ordination in Innsbruck. Dad, in particular, seemed overjoyed that he had two sons ordained priests. His joy reflected that of our grandparents, John and Anna Penaskovic. As a teenager Anna had worked cooking meals and doing housekeeping for the village priest in Mala Lodina, Slovakia. She had a great deal of respect for the clergy. In fact, she gave us $600.00 to have custom made chalices for our celebration of the first Mass. These beautiful chalices were designed and made by a respectable goldsmith in Schweinfurt, Germany.

In the months leading up to ordination Father Walter Hof, Cleric Master at the friary in Wuerzburg, gave Richie pointers on the rubrics to be followed in celebrating Mass. The Second Vatican Council's decree on the Liturgy enjoined that the Mass be said in the vernacular language, in this case, German, although at the twins' first Mass in Wuerzburg, many of the prayers were still recited in Latin.

OUR FIRST MASS IN WUERZBURG, GERMANY

We celebrated not one but two first Masses. Our classmate, John Burkhard, celebrated the first one with us in the environs of Innsbruck in an old-age home. The elderly were not accustomed to the Mass in the vernacular, in this case, German, nor were they savvy in regard to the subtleties of the liturgy. At the offertory of the Mass where one puts one's host on the paten prior to the consecration, the folks at the old age home put coins in the chalice, much to our astonishment.

The Franciscan church in Wuerzburg marked the site of our *Primiz* or First Mass in Germany. A large crowd of people packed the Franciscan church for the High Mass complete with incense and five celebrants. We were so nervous that we mumbled through the opening prayers in Latin. After Mass we had an elaborate banquet for about thirty people, including a Jewish couple, Richard and his wife, Janet Zimmerman who studied medicine at the University of Wuerzburg, Germany and Ivan Allison, a member of the Green Berets or Special Forces. Ivan had been a student at Trenton Catholic High School where he knew many of the Conventual friars who staffed this institution. He and Rich became good friends at Wuerzburg.

MEETING POPE PAUL VI

In the days after ordination Dad, Bob and I flew to Rome, Italy for an audience with Pope Paul VI in Rome. The former Rector of the minor seminary, Father Sebastian Weber, had arranged for the papal audience. He knew the papal Master of Ceremonies, an Italian bishop, and kept it as a surprise for Bob and Rich. Little did we know when we joined the thousands of pilgrims jammed into St. Peter's Basilica to see the Pope, that we would actually shake hands with the Supreme Pontiff.

When we arrived at St. Peter's Basilica thousands of the faithful filled this fabulous church. Father Sebastian told us to follow him. Led into the sanctuary, we were joined by about 15 other newly ordained priests from all over the world. The Pope said a few words in Italian to those gathered in St. Peter's cavernous basilica. He then came down to the newly ordained and shook hands personally with each of us. As the pope approached us, Bob asked me if he could offer the pope an American cigarette. I laughed and said the pope could buy his own American cigarettes if he were so disposed.

Our pictures were taken with the Pontiff and the official Vatican newspaper, *L'Osservatore Romano* commented on our papal audience. We introduced Dad and our cousin, Helen Gala, to the Pope. We received a congratulatory telegram from Cardinal Cicognani, the Vatican Secretary of State. We then said a first Mass at St. Peter's Basilica on one of the side altars in the crypt underneath the basilica.

VISIT TO YUGOSLAVIA

From Rome we left by train for Sremska Mitrovica in Yugoslavia, located about an hour by train from Belgrade, the capital. Dense settlement took place in the central Balkan Peninsula until about 7000–3,500 B.C. E. during the Neolithic Period. After 3,500 B.C.E. semi-nomadic pastoral peoples infiltrated this region. They migrated southward form the Russian steppes and were speakers of Indo-European languages. They domesticated horses, used horse-drawn vehicles, and their extensive trade routes carried bronze, gold, and amber. This made their military technology superior to others at the time.

The Romans expanded into the Balkan Peninsula in the late 3rd century B.C.E. They searched for copper, iron, precious metals, crops, and slaves. Actually, Roman conquest served to stimulate both migration and cultural assimilation. Roman influence weakened gradually in the face of incursions by Avars, Bulgars, Goths, and Huns.

From the 1st to the 6th century Sremska Mitrovica, known then as Sirmium, served as the administrative center of the Roman province of Pannonia Secunda. In the early Christian period both the imperial residence and the bishop's see were located in Sirmium. Between the 3rd and the 4th century the city functioned as the center of the governors of the province and the seat of the Roman prefecture of Illyricum. Archaeological evidence suggests that Sirmium contained the Emperor's palace, the necropolis, surrounded by moats and ramparts, the hippodrome, baths, and craft centers.

When we visited Sremska Mitrovica in 1967 there were about one hundred Penaskovics living there. We stayed with Adam, the brother of our grandfather, John, on Dad's side of the family and his wife, Katherina. Adam seemed to keep folks at a distance, not only strangers but also family members. His wife, Katherina, his polar opposite, struck us as warm and friendly, and made us feel right at home.

They had four pigs, thirty chickens, and twenty-five small chicks in an incubator inside the kitchen of their home which had no central heating. One had to put on special wooden shoes to walk through the mud in order to use the outhouse. Instead of toilet paper one had to use cut-up, strips of newspapers. They certainly did the trick. Today that has all changed. Sremska Mitrovica has all the conveniences of modern day living.

The city had a population of about 35,000 most of whom were Serbs. The Catholic church of St. Demetrius had 5,000 parishioners, but the spirit of the people might be characterized as weak according to the pastor. During the Early Byzantine period Sirmium became the center of the cult of St. Demeterios, the protector of the city of Salonica. That's probably why the church bore the name St. Demetrius.

Ten to fifteen percent of the Catholics pledged allegiance to the Communist Party. What did it mean to be communist? It meant that one did not go to church not even to baptize one's children. One could not rise in the communist system unless one became a member of the Communist Party. Our cousin, Ilya, a school teacher, could never become principal of the school unless he joined the Communist Party and gave up his religion. The liturgical renewal inaugurated by the Second Vatican Council revived the people's spirit according to the pastor of St. Demetrius.

The city boasted of its sugar factory along with its beer factory. Built on the ruins of the old Roman city of Sirmium, the Sava River coursed through the town. These were the days of communism and a large photo of Tito, surrounded by flowers, caught our eye. The communist government posted it prominently in every major store or else store owners felt they had to display it prominently so as to curry favor with the communists. For all outward appearances one would think that Tito resembled one of the Roman gods. Back then people wondered what would happen to Yugoslavia once Tito died. "How would the country hold together," they asked? That turned out to be a very legitimate question as the country faced a severe crisis after Tito's death.

Yugoslavia practiced a cold, lukewarm type of communism. At the border the guards did not even open our passports once they recognized that we were Americans. They welcomed tourists particularly from the U.S. because they were a boon to the economy.

We visited in the cold of winter with no central heating in our relatives' house. Before going to sleep they would put heated bricks in our beds to keep our feet warm. With no central heating the bedrooms were so cold in the morning that one could hang meat. The Slovak remedy consisted in the ingestion of two shots of whisky as a quick "get me upper." Katherine, the wife of Adam woke us up by offering us two shots of Slivovitz before we got out of bed in the morning, much to our surprise and delight. That certainly managed to get our adrenaline going.

At that time the streets of Sremska Mitrovica were unpaved. The "taxi" consisted of a horse-drawn carriage pulling us through the streets of the city.

In spots the mud reached a depth of eighteen inches, but the horse had no
trouble getting us down to the train station, teeming with people at 6:30 in
the morning. Folks were already enjoying a liquid breakfast, much to our
astonishment. We then flew back to Innsbruck from Belgrade. Bob returned
to the States and Richie continued his studies in Wuerzburg.

After ordination, I took the train down to Munich and arranged to visit
Professor Heinrich Fries, the best known Newman scholar in West Germany
at the time. I asked Fries if I could come to Munich and write my dissertation
on Newman under his direction. Fries said "Yes," and I jumped for joy. He
told me to send the results of the *Hauptpruefung* to the Dean of the Faculty
of Theology at Munich, so that I could be admitted to the doctoral program
in theology at the Ludwig Maximilians Universitaet Muenchen. I did this and
shortly thereafter received a letter informing me that I could do my doctoral
studies at Munich under the direction of Professor Heinrich Fries.

Professor Fries, a student of Joseph Geiselmann at Tuebingen, wrote his
doctoral dissertation on Newman's philosophy of religion, receiving the
doctorate *summa cum laude* back in 1942 when the Nazi party still called
the shots in Germany. Named parochial vicar for the area of Tuebingen, Dr.
Fries daily rode his bicycle as far as twenty miles to take care of the spiritual
needs of his congregation. The Nazis did not allow Fries to get gas for his
little motorcycle since the Nazis did not see pastoral work as a necessary part
of the war effort. A Nazi official asserted that the Church should be glad that
it had been left in peace.

The Catholic theological faculty at the University of Tuebingen invited Fries
to write a post-doctoral dissertation called a *Habilitationsschrift*, which was
necessary to become a professor at a German university. Fries became professor of fundamental theology at Tuebingen in 1950, after serving as a lecturer
in theology since 1946. Fries received a *Ruf* or invitation to become professor
of fundamental theology in Munich where he had seminars on such Newman
classics as *An Essay on the Development of Christian Doctrine*, the *Idea of
a University* and on *An Essay in aid of a Grammar of Assent*. It was quite an
honor to get a call to become a member of another theological faculty.

Fries also received an offer to become a professor at the University of
Muenster in 1963 but turned it down when the University of Munich offered
to make him Director of the Institute for Ecumenical Theology. The Institute
would receive money to build up its theological library and had space where
doctoral seminars could be held. The Institute was conveniently located about
two blocks from the main part of the university on Schellingstrasse. In the
early 1960s Fries received an offer to become a *peritus* or theological advisor to Cardinal Doepfner at the Second Vatican council but turned down this
invitation, a decision he later regretted.

HOMEWARD BOUND

After successfully passing the Hauptpruefung, the Provincial asked me to return to the U.S. I received orders to go to St. Joseph's Church in Hoboken, New Jersey from Thanksgiving to January 3rd, 1968. St. Joe's ministered to the Hispanic population. Our weekly collection amounted to around $200.00. Many people put in a handful of pennies into the collection basket.

Father Richard, the associate pastor of the parish, had spent some time in Costa Rica and knew Spanish well. He looked after the pastoral needs of the Spanish-speaking members of the parish who made up about 80% of the parishioners. Rough around the edges, he tended to respect me for whatever reason. I once held a service called Benediction and he assisted me. A chair stood in our way as we were processing in the sacristy in front of the congregation. Father Richard just flat-out kicked the chair out of our way, much to my amazement.

Hoboken at that time had a reputation for being a tough city, one that was well-deserved. An Italian gentleman who lived across the street from the rectory gave me a hard time and I mentioned this to Father Richard. Father Richard worked with the Hispanic population in Hoboken and said to me. "Rich, if you want I can have that man's Cadillac disappear without a trace. And the police won't ever find it." I could not believe my ears. I said "No, I'll just live with it."

We would get our share of obscene phone calls in the rectory. I remember being propositioned by a hooker as I waited for a traffic light to change about one block from the rectory. Sometimes people would phone us only to curse us out. This did not upset me. I figured this kind of treatment went along with the job.

Actually, I loved parish ministry in Hoboken, a city located only about a fifteen minute ride by car from my home town of Bayonne, I had numerous occasions to visit my parents. One day a strikingly glamorous girl with long, beautiful brown hair, knocked on the rectory door and asked if she could make her First Communion. I almost passed out. I asked her what she did for a living and her answer startled me. "I'm a go-go dancer in Manhattan," she said calmly. I tried not to show it but inwardly I was flabbergasted. Over the next few weeks, I instructed her in the faith, heard her first confession, and gave her first Communion. I felt that I had done something worthwhile in my life. This small event made my twelve hard years of study worthwhile.

My superiors in the Franciscan Order then asked me to teach religion at Canevin High School in Pittsburgh. Located in the suburbs, this school bore the name of the fifth Bishop of Pittsburgh, John Canevin, who governed the diocese from 1853–1920. The Rev. Gervase Beyer, whom we had known as our Latin and logic teacher at St. Francis Minor Seminary, had been named Headmaster in 1962. The friars seemed to have a love-hate relationship with Father Gervase. He could be stern but deep down had a soft spot in his heart for the downtrodden. Frankly, I worshiped the ground he walked on.

Father Gervase, A.K.A. "Jerry," had a German shepherd dog that guarded the hallway leading into his room. The dog tended to be aggressive and would often bare his teeth to those who approached Jerry's room. I befriended the dog, and on occasion, took it outside for walks. The high school had over 2,000 students, both male and female. I taught five classes of religion a day and found this to be the most enervating job I ever had. By the late afternoon I often wound up sleeping until supper time in a lounge chair in my room. Sometimes the students would drink beer for breakfast and come to school with a buzz. I found this to be disheartening because they then had to be dismissed for the day and missed out on their academic work.

The mood of the friary at Canevin left something to be desired. Some of the friars resented Gervase's dog, which they may have regarded as a projection of Jerry himself. I had my own set of problems, namely, maintaining discipline in the classroom. I loved teaching but on the high school level at least, one had to be half a cop. The students were delightful, but I did not feel close to the lay faculty. Jerry made me advisor to the chess club, although I did not care to play chess myself. On weekends I said Mass in neighboring parishes and found this to be a fulfilling part of my ministry. Thankfully, my stay at Canevin lasted only from January to June of 1968.

BOB AS HOSPITAL CHAPLAIN

After returning from Europe we celebrated another first Mass at St. Joseph's Church in Bayonne, New Jersey on November 19th, 1967. Hundreds of parishioners turned out for this event. The pastor, Msgr. Chmely arranged for a reception for us from 2:00 to 4:00 P.M. in the parish hall at which time parishioners formed long lines to receive our first blessing. Dad and Mom were ecstatic. Dad's pride caused the buttons on his shirt to pop off.

I completed my internship at Our Lady of Angels Church in Albany, New York. I counseled clients under the careful supervision of Fr. Jeffrey Keefe, a clinical psychologist. I also completed all the requirements for the Master's degree in theology except for the thesis. My Franciscan superiors assigned me to St. Francis Medical Center in Trenton, New Jersey as Chaplain. Father Timothy Lyons, pastor of Immaculate Conception Church requested that I work at St. Francis Hospital.

The work can best be described in one word, "grueling," physically, psychologically, and emotionally. I taught an ethics course at the school of nursing, gave daily sermons, counseled hospital staff and patients, and visited each new hospital admission. On call 24 hours a day, I responded to all hospital emergency codes in order to administer last rites to the dying. In addition, the medical doctors, taking the easy way out, relied on us to break the news to family members that their loved one had died. My emotions ran out after telling parents that their young child had died.

I hardly ever got a full night's sleep. I would be paged to go to the Intensive Care Unit or to the emergency room about every night. My day began at 5:00 A.M. After Mass, I distributed Holy Communion to the entire hospital so that by 9:00 A.M. exhaustion would hit me like a clothesline. During this time I became friends with Sr. Marie Thomas, Director of Nurses, who had responsibility for 1100 employees of the hospital. Apart from our shared interest in religious life and in reading poetry, we both enjoyed reading *The New York Times* on Sunday. She eventually left the hospital for graduate studies in Washington, D.C.

In August of 1968 Fr. Timothy asked me to be the associate pastor at Immaculate Conception parish in Trenton. His director of youth ministry was reassigned and he wanted me to take over the job. I received a formal letter from my Major Superior and Bishop Ahr of Trenton informing me of this request. I began work as Director of Youth Ministry, running the religious education program for students who attended public schools and directing the liturgical program of the parish.

Immaculate Conception Church had been established in 1875 to cater to the needs of immigrants of German and Irish descent. In the Sixties 5,000 families belonged to this parish, the majority of whom were of Italian descent. Five Conventual Franciscan priests were assigned to this parish. The parish had an active and engaged laity and a lay board that administered the sports program. To give you an idea of the size of this parish, we had 18 basketball teams in the Catholic Youth Organization (C.Y.O.). Our dances attracted 400 teenagers a week and our junior Holy Name Society had 100 teenage boys. In sum, we had, indeed, a vibrant parish.

I greatly desired to earn a master's degree in pastoral counseling at nearby Princeton Theological Seminary to beef up my counseling skills. However, the pastor, Father Timothy, turned down my request saying that I had too much to do in the parish. Greatly disappointed, I realized that I did the lion's share of work in the parish. Other friars stationed there resented the fact that I engaged the parishioners in doing psychological counseling. They could see spiritual direction as an important part of a priest's work, not however, professional counseling.

The topic of race relations rankled them. The parish composed mostly of Italian Catholics had some parishioners who were uncomfortable with blacks. There were tense confrontations between the white parishioners and the blacks who they felt were encroaching on their neighborhood. This led in the Sixties to demonstrations and mini-riots carried on the local (Philadelphia) news. The newly-elected black Superintendent of Schools for Trenton named me to the citizens' advisory committee for race relations. As much as possible, I endeavored to keep in line some of our youngsters who had difficulty dealing with blacks.

DISENCHANTMENT SETS IN

In May of 1969 I participated in a forum at Rutgers University on birth control. A member of Planned Parenthood also spoke and I agreed with his thesis that the individual must decide in good conscience whether or not to practice birth control. Not surprisingly, the Papal Commission, comprised of the top moral theologians in the world, (including Alfons Auer, Richie's professor at Wuerzburg), came to the same identical conclusion. Pope Paul set up this Committee or blue ribbon panel of moral theologians for the express purpose of determining the morality of artificial contraception. The Pope, instead of following the majority report of his Commission, went with the minority view in his 1968 encyclical, *Humanae Vitae*. This action resulted in a storm of protest throughout the Catholic world. I felt badly that the Church placed such a terrible burden on the laity.

In June of 1969 the pastor of Immaculate Conception Church, Fr. Tim Lyons, put me in charge of the garbage for the annual summer fair of the parish. This fair raised about $70,000 for the parish. I felt that I was being punished by this action. Combined with my deep disappointment over not attending Princeton Theological Seminary's pastoral counseling program, I decided to leave the active ministry. Looking back, I believe God had delivered me a telegram stating, "This is my will for you."

I met with my pastor, informing him of my decision. I handed over the keys to the parish car as well as my American Express card and gasoline credit card. I left with a mere $5.00 in my pocket. I stayed with my brother, Bill, and his wife in nearby New Brunswick, New Jersey. For the next several years I lived the vow of poverty in an existential way. For the first time in my life, I knew first-hand what the vow of poverty really entailed.

BEGINNING FROM SCRATCH

In leaving the Franciscan order, and any religious order for that matter, in the Sixties, several factors worked against me. First, I had no money and could not get even a gasoline credit card. I had no paid employment history except for summer jobs. It was as if I had been living on Mars the past thirteen years. Second, I had no job. I did, however, possess skills such as experience in counseling.

Third, some family members did not take kindly to my decision to leave the Franciscans and the active ministry. Dad took my decision to leave extremely hard. My grandmother could not understand it at all. She felt terribly let down, particularly since she held the priesthood in such high regard. Although Richie had doubts of his own at this time, nevertheless, he told Dad he would stay a priest so as to reassure him that there would be at least one priest in the Penaskovic family.

RICHIE STRUGGLES

My doubts took the form of questions which I recorded in my diary at that time. I felt that I could have a greater impact on the world as a priest than in any other profession I might choose. "I've seen Christ work through me in the confessional and in preaching." So I wrote in my journal entry on December 12, 1969. I believed that "God will see me through." I repeated many times in my mind the Old Testament words in Latin, *Ego ero tecum*, (I, meaning God, shall be with you"). I felt called like Samuel to be a listener, a hearer of the word. When God called, Samuel's answer reverberated in my ear, "Speak, Yahweh, your servant is listening."

I remember reading about a poet I greatly admired, Gerard Manley Hopkins. Physical debility often made him depressed, yet he recalled Peter's words, "To whom shall I go? You have the words of eternal life." Hopkins noted that "I would gladly live my life in great or greater seclusion from the world and be busied only with God." I agreed with Hopkins.

My theological hero, Karl Rahner, influenced me greatly in my decision to remain a Franciscan and a priest. Rahner stated that whoever makes profession as a religious binds himself irrevocably to a way of life and a destiny one cannot know in advance. The consequences of such a risky undertaking can be difficult. To undertake such a bold adventure requires guts. However, without this kind of daring, there's no giving of oneself to a cause larger than oneself. Without this giving of oneself to another, one remains stuck in selfishness, anxious about one's being.

To be a priest, says Rahner, means to be thrown hither and fro, this way and that. One receives a gash in the side, yet by means of this wound one gets a glimpse into the Infinite, the Eternal. These were the thoughts swimming in my brain after Bob left the Franciscans. Unfortunately, my doubts continued.

SUMMER IN MONTREAL

The summer of 1970 saw me ministering to a German parish in the Portuguese section of Montreal off Saint Laurent Avenue on a street called Hotel de Ville. People came to Sunday Mass, in this the only German parish in Montreal, from all corners of this beautiful city. Like Luther, I preached in German on the gospel of the day. The people of this parish warmly accepted me. The other priest stationed with me, Fr. Germain Williams, had been for many years the former Cleric Master at St. Anthony on Hudson, the major seminary of the Conventual Franciscans located outside of Albany, New York. Fr. Germain bet me $25.00 I would not last two more years as a Franciscan. I proved him wrong but forgot to collect my debt.

I hit it off particularly well with the young people of the parish who could relate to me as one of their contemporaries. I played football, tennis, basketball, and ping pong with them. They were happy to have a priest with whom they could relate and tell their problems. At this time there were tensions in Montreal between the English and the French and the group known as the Quebecquois, which occasionally placed bombs in mailboxes as a protest on the part of a small minority of the French, who resented the dominance of the English language in Canada.

One day my brother, Tommy, telephoned and asked to visit me along with his friend, Ray Burner, a star baseball pitcher at St. Mary's in Jersey City, New Jersey. Ray had a 90 M.P.H. fastball and could have, with proper coaching and discipline, made the major leagues. While in Montreal and staying at the rectory, Ray brought along some marihuana. This involved taking a huge risk, particularly in a foreign country. My Franciscan superiors would hardly be amused had the police found marihuana in the parish rectory.

One summer evening my brother, Tom, and I visited a German beer hall and were returning home around 2:00 A.M. The streets were as barren as a tree in the Arctic. Four men stood around the corner from the rectory. Two were in their Forties and two were around twenty. I said to Tommy, "Let's cross the street and walk right in front of them." As we walked by, one of the younger men flinched.

I said to Tommy, "Isn't it strange that one of them flinched because they outnumbered us two to one." As I put the key in the rectory door I noticed that one of them glanced around the corner of the building as we were about to enter the rectory. This struck me as strange. I said to Tom, "They must be up to something."

We went into the rectory and I said "Let's stay up and see what happens." A few minutes later one of the men opened the mailbox of the rectory and peeked in, apparently to see if there were lights on and we were still up. I said to Tommy, I'm going to call the cops." He said, "Let's wait and see." A few minutes later we heard the sound of glass breaking and I said to Tommy, "That's it." I telephoned the police.

The police arrived almost instantaneously with their service revolvers out. They determined that the electronics store next to us had been vandalized. The Montreal police took down my name and number. The next day two detectives arrived at the rectory and interviewed me. They wanted an accurate description of the four men. We were able to give a good description and the detectives told us that this gang was well known for having burglarized many places throughout the city. About two weeks later I read in the papers that the police caught this gang of hoodlums, much to my relief.

A FISH OUT OF WATER

I taught theology on the graduate level in the fall of 1970 at the major seminary of the Conventual Franciscans in Rensselaer, New York, St. Anthony on Hudson. Instead of teaching my specialty, fundamental theology, I taught "Bibliography and Methods of Research," and another course on "Karl Barth, Rudolf Bultmann, and Dietrich Bonhoeffer." It bothered me greatly that I could not teach my specialty, fundamental theology. Instead, Father Patrick Gallagher who specialized in Scripture Studies, taught it and judging from students' comments, did less than a brilliant job.

Patrick confided to me that he and Father Peter Damian did not want me to teach fundamental theology because the theology at St. Anthony on Hudson had two orientations: Franciscan and conservative. It became increasingly clear to me that the theology I had been taught in Germany did not sit well for those educated in Rome, namely, Fr. Patrick and Fr. Peter Damian. I wrote this entry in my journal" "I think the students were cheated. Here I could have done a smashing job of teaching fundamental theology and yet my superiors denied me the opportunity of doing so. This all upsets me very much."

During this time my doubts about my vocation to religious life and to the priesthood intensified. I felt like a fish out of water. I perceived a yawning chasm between my intellectual formation and that of my conferees in the Franciscan Order. How thrilled I was to return to Munich to continue writing my dissertation on John Henry Newman. However, in Munich I continued to struggle with loneliness.

THE U.S. EMBASSY IN MUNICH

After ordination I (Richie) pursued the Ph.D. degree in theology at the Ludwig Maximilians Universitaet Muenchen, better known as the University of Munich, a large institution with over 34,000 students in 1968. On the weekend I worked as a Civilian Chaplain for the U.S. Army, Europe in Murnau, Garmisch, the recreational area for U.S. forces in Germany, and Oberammergau, site of the famous passion play put on every decade. I said Mass for the troops, heard confessions, and learned to do counseling by the seat of my pants.

The commanding officer of the base would, on occasion, send difficult cases to me. Once he sent me a soldier handcuffed and escorted by two military policemen. The soldier appeared to have suicidal tendencies and the colonel of the base wanted me to decide what to do with this seriously depressed G.I. At first blush, I felt keenly the terrible responsibility thrust on me but I possessed oodles of common sense. I discovered that I had to listen very carefully and attempt to detect the source of this soldier's problem.

This soldier, in particular, had a 140 I.Q. and the Army assigned him to clean toilets all day. I recommended he have a change of assignment. Some months later I ran into him and he was a changed person. He assisted the regular Army chaplain and was quite content in his work and in his life, telling me that no one ever took the trouble to hear him out the way I did. I learned that I was adept at establishing rapport with all kinds of troubled individuals.

Although I had an exciting life as a priest, I struggled with the problem of loneliness. I co-directed a small group of Roman Catholics who met for Mass each Sunday at the Jesuit house on the Kaulbacherstrasse in Munich. Brian Mc Dermott, a Jesuit, and I said Mass for the group. We were a motley crew: Moira Elegant, a millionaire from Australia, the wife of Bob Elegant, then a syndicated columnist for *The Los Angeles Times* and an expert on China. (He would go on to write the best-selling novel, *Dynasty*); several individuals from Radio Free Europe from Eastern bloc countries, like Czechoslovakia, an artist from Italy; several Irish lasses, who moved to Germany in search of a job and husband in that order; an executive for a leading semi-conductor company who won a gold medal at the Winter Olympics in Helsinki in 1961; and an officer with U.S.Army, Europe along with his wife from St. Paul, Minnesota, among others.

Because of these contacts I received invitations to parties at the U.S. Embassy in Munich. As a priest I felt welcome in all kinds of society and this thrilled me. I once attended an all night Mardi Gras party called in German, "Fasching" at the upscale Hotel Europaischer Hof in the heart of Munich. Dick Murphy, the executive for a semi-conductor company, who was about six feet four inches tall, came dressed as Snow White and I posed as one of the seven dwarfs. We had such a fun time.

LONELY IN LONDON

From the end of 1971 I lay on my death-bed, as regards my membership in the Franciscan Order, though at that time I became aware of it only gradually. As John Henry Newman observes in his *Apologia Pro Vita Sua*, a death-bed scarcely has a history. Rather, it's a tedious decline with alternating rallying and falling back. It is a season when doors are shut and curtains drawn, one in which the sick person cannot record the stages of his illness.

For Christmas in 1971 I jetted to London to do research on my dissertation at the British Museum. I used the money I earned from the military to finance my trip. I stayed with the Conventual Franciscans in the Waterloo section of the city and met the actress, Ann Sheridan, who regularly attended Mass there. I loved visiting the Soho district, shopping on Oxford Street, and making a side trip to Oxford to work in the famous Bodleian Library.

On December, 1971 I mustered up enough nerve to make the transatlantic call to Nancy Hare and tell her that I loved her. She had been on my mind for several days and I felt compelled to call her. I had not known her that well, having met her briefly on four occasions. Nancy, a Sister of Mercy, was taking a shower when I called. Although completely flabbergasted by my call, she did not brush me off because I hardly knew her. Instead, she answered in her own diplomatic way, "Rich, we'll talk about it when you return from Europe." I took her answer as a "Yes."

I would describe Nancy as a caring and feeling person. I was attracted to her the first time we had met. I had said Mass at an apartment complex in a rough section of Albany, New York and Nancy attended, along with some other sisters. I knew intuitively that she was the right person for me. Although tempted to fly home and see her in person, my twin, Bob, dissuaded me from this and told me to finish my doctorate first. I took his shrewd advice and finished writing the dissertation in 1972. I then studied nine months for the comprehensive exams which I took in January of 1973. This exam lasted two hours and took place entirely in German before the Dean of the Theological Faculty and three professors. To my amazement I received the doctorate degree, *magna cum laude*, jumping two feet off the ground when I heard the news. God had indeed come through for me.

A TUG OF WAR

I then flew back to New York. I informed my superiors in the Franciscan Order about my decision to leave. One of them suggested that it would be sinful to leave. They provided psychological counseling in hopes that I might change my mind. A tug of war took place in the narrow confines of my heart. After all, I had gone off to the Franciscans when but fifteen years old. I had spent seventeen years a Franciscan and loved them, and continue to love them.

I felt as strong a call to leave religious life as I had received in entering the Order. I did not know why God demanded this of me. I saw the strong hands of the Lord in the events of my life. In the thirty years since I made the decision to leave, I have never looked back, never for once doubting the wisdom of my decision. I did not leave simply to get married. Other factors loomed large.

All kinds of turmoil raged within the Catholic Church at the time, all as a result of Vatican II. My own theological views had become much more liberal ever since I entered the Canisianum in 1963. I imbibed the theology of Vatican II almost by osmosis from the intellectual atmosphere in which I lived and studied in Austria and Germany. When I returned to the States in 1973, my Franciscan confreres were still living theologically in the pre-Vatican II days, and saw me as a fish out of water. They doubted my orthodoxy. Several times when sent to preach, the pastor would be listening to what I said to see that it was theologically kosher. I found this very disturbing.

I also had this dilemma. As a priest the laity had the expectation that I would tell them the church's views on the morality of contraception, homosexuality, and divorce. I did not always agree with the church on these issues. Yet, as a member of the clergy, I had an obligation to present the official teaching of the Church. This I could not, in good conscience, do. I felt compelled to leave the active ministry in order to be true to myself. I felt like Martin Luther declaring, "Here I stand, I can do no other."

In leaving the active ministry I thought of myself as functioning like an off-duty trooper with the whole world as my jurisdiction, alert to where I might intervene to exercise my ministry. I still think of myself as a priest, but one on special assignment. I feel less conspicuous now without the Roman collar. I feel liberated, able to act as a force for good in the world.

BOB GETS HIS BEARINGS

A number of priests and religious were leaving the ministry in 1969 and several organizations emerged that helped former priests make the transition to the lay state. One of these organizations called itself Bearings in New York City.

Bearings helped me (Bob) secure employment in the Westchester County probation Department. The Franciscans loaned me $1,500 to kick-start my life in the secular world. I used part of that money for a down payment on a car. Within a year's time I paid back my loan to the Franciscans. Meanwhile, I moved to Odessa, New York. Soon afterwards I looked up my friend, Theresa Conaty who, unbeknown to me, had left the convent and was living in New York City.

Soon we began dating. In September, 1969 I moved to White Plains, New York to work with the Westchester County Probation Department. I handled writs of habeas corpus that were referred from the Supreme Court to the Family Court. I loved working in the adoption unit.

Theresa and I found that we were good friends and shared many common interests. We continued to date and decided to get married over Christmas vacation in Veteran, New York on Dec. 20, 1969. At the time Theresa worked at Morisania hospital in the Bronx and lived at the Bridge apartments on 178th street in Manhattan. She took a position as Assistant Director of Nursing in Long Beach, New York. To my great delight I discovered I could transfer to the Nassau County Probation Department, which was close to Long Beach.

My family did not take kindly to my departure from the Franciscans and from the active priestly ministry. Dad refused to attend my wedding. My grandmother was brokenhearted. Some family members and friends thought that I had broken a sacred trust. My twin in Germany at the time supported me in my decision wholeheartedly, as did Mom.

Meanwhile, the administrator of Long Beach Hospital gave us the name of a competent real estate broker who could secure a home rental after we returned from our honeymoon in Venezuela. Our first home on Pt. Lookout, Long Island had eight rooms, two bathrooms and two working fireplaces. Fully furnished, the owners Jack and Elizabeth Kane treated us like family and became lifelong friends. The winter rental came to $125 per month; in summer it went up to $1,500. In April we moved into another rental property for May and June. Then we signed a two year lease with an option to buy. In 1971 we purchased our first home. Our neighbors, Sal and Vicki Palestro loaned us $10,000 interest free so we could buy this home for $29,000. We survived on one paycheck for a year and paid them back within the first year of ownership along with an expensive gift.

COUNTING OUR BLESSINGS

1. Ordination, the culmination of years of discipline and study, made us feel special. After all, not even the angels can change ordinary bread and wine into the Body and Blood of Christ as can a priest, acting in and through the power of Jesus.
2. How privileged we were to be able to shake hands with and have our pictures taken with the Pope. Not many people can say that, particularly nowadays when heightened security remains the order of the day.
3. We found it gratifying to hear confessions and to absolve people of their sins in the name of Christ. We did not look upon hearing confessions as a chore. Rather, it reminded us of our own sinfulness and unworthiness in the sight of God. It made us humble knowing that, except for the grace of God, there go I.

Chapter Six

The Way of Knowledge
and the Way of Empathy

". . . there is a place deep inside where one's real life goes on, much like an underground river in parched, dry country, which flows whether one knows about it or not."

Sharon Bustle

"I left the woods for as good a reason as I went there. Perhaps it seemed to me that I had several lives to live, and could not spare any more time for that one."

Henry David Thoreau

The aforementioned quote from Thoreau sums up how we felt after leaving the "woods," that is, the Franciscans. In a sense we who were caterpillars would now be changed into butterflies now that we were on our own. Just as we felt God called us to the religious life, so too, did we have the conviction that we were called to leave the Franciscans in response to a call dialed from a heavenly phone.

Yet in our new lives we would embark on distinct but parallel paths. Richie Blue would take the path of knowledge spending the rest of his life in academia; Bobby Brown would go into private practice helping his clients deal with their problems both personal and relational. Richie would use his language skills to do research and, hopefully, teach his students how to find wisdom. Bob would, in turn, be empathetic to the struggles of the human heart, teaching his clients how to be whole.

RICHIE ON THE WAY OF KNOWLEDGE

I left the Franciscans in June of 1973 with heavy heart and a total of $1,000 given me by the Franciscans. I left with no job, no car, no credit cards, and no place to live. For the first time in his life I truly imitated St. Francis, living the life of poverty in an existential way. Priests who exited the priesthood in the Sixties and Seventies were pretty much given the bum's rush with barely the clothes on their back. They would face rejection both by many family members and by friends. I would be no exception to such a fate.

To be a priest meant to have instant status. One had immediate respect from one's family and friends. One day I drove over the Goethals Bridge near Elizabeth, New Jersey and realized I made a mistake and wanted to turn around. I had my Roman collar on and told the cop at the toll booth what I had in mind. He got out of the booth and stopped the traffic in both directions so I could make an illegal U turn. That Roman collar certainly came in handy that day.

Many of the laity thought that those who left the priesthood were failures. One also had to deal with job discrimination. Item: I applied for a position at a Catholic college in the Midwest. They were very interested in my application until they found out that I had left the priesthood. Then, I suddenly became of no interest to them. Item: *The National Catholic Reporter*, a prominent national Catholic newspaper, had an ad for an Executive Director of Pastoral Studies in the Diocese of Green Bay, Wisconsin. I applied for the position but again when they learned that I had a leave of absence from the priesthood they, too, became uninterested in pursuing my application.

I found such discrimination discouraging. I could not get a job in the Diocese of Ogdensburg, New York as Coordinator of Religious Education because of my background. Yet, as I found out years later, these same dioceses were treating priests in the active ministry who were pedophiles and ephebophiles with kid gloves. Their bishops were simply reassigning them to other parishes. Even after conviction these priests were given a pension with a guaranteed income.

How did this make me feel? I felt discouraged, depressed, and worried about my future. I remember applying for jobs in Washington, D.C. where there were over 700 applicants for one position. I rejoiced if I were lucky enough to get a letter of rejection or one acknowledging I had even applied for the job. Don't get me wrong. Job discrimination did not only extend to church-related positions. I interviewed for a staff position at Union College in Schenectady, New York. The interviewee said that "I would have the job in a heart-beat if I were black." This also discouraged me, because I had no control over the color of my skin.

The example of my twin kept me going at that time. After all, he had weathered a similar storm and came out with flying colors. He had bought his first house in Pt. Lookout, N.Y., adopted two children, and had a respectable job as Senior Probation officer for Nassau County. I knew that I had a "soul friend" in Bobby Brown who ran through the same obstacle course I was facing and came up grinning.

Soon after leaving the Franciscans in June of 1973, I went to live at the Franciscan Renewal Center in Scottsdale, Arizona. These were the Brown Franciscans, the Order of Friars Minor, and were most kind to me. Father Barry, in particular, allowed me to use to stay at the Renewal Center free of charge. He let me borrow his car while I tried to find a job in Phoenix.

I found the heat oppressive. It would be 105 degrees in the shade on many a summer day. I could not find a job. I got a free ride to San Diego through the California desert with another Franciscan and hitchhiked from San Diego to Oakland in search of work but came up empty.

There were some scary moments. In San Diego I met a man, named Bill, at a convention sponsored by Catholic Charismatics. He was a huge, strapping man about 6 feet four inches with an orange sweatshirt with cigarette burns in it. Bill was driving an orange Volkswagen to Oakland and said I could travel with him and another man. This other person started talking to himself, which made me uneasy. However, the man who talked to himself exited the car before it got out of the San Diego city limits telling me that Bill "had several cards short of a full deck." That left me and this "crazy man" together for the long ride to Oakland.

I sat upfront and, lo and behold, on the passenger side were two large cans of gasoline, about 15 gallons worth. If we had had a crash, I would be history. Bill spoke non-stop for the first four hours of the trip. At one point I told Bill that we were almost on empty and we would soon run out of gas. Sure enough we ran out of gas. Bill then stopped and refueled as huge trucks passed within 18 inches of our car, shaking the ground as they roared by.

I volunteered to do some of the driving but Bill pointed out that some of the controls had to be operated by string. He then asked if I knew how to pull the various strings. I answered "No." He then stated that I could not drive the car. At times Bill would be doing 45 M.P.H. in a 65 M.P.H. zone in the passing lane of the California freeway. There would be a long trail of cars behind us. As they passed us they made obscene jesters, which did not faze Bill in the least but which left me horrified. Relief came when we pulled into a rough section of Oakland, California at 1:00 A.M. I went into the hotel, locked the door, and said a prayer of thanksgiving.

I could not find any suitable employment in the Oakland/San Francisco area. I applied in person at a number of colleges but nothing panned out. I then took a Greyhound bus from San Francisco to Phoenix. The jobs in Phoenix paid terrible wages. Hence at the end of the summer I flew back east to Schenectady, New York.

I learned that Cousin Dora Bolger with whom I had lived from ages nine to seventeen had been in a hospital with complications from diabetes. Before Cousin Dora entered the hospital she had her daughter, Doris, call many people for the last time in order to say "Goodbye." Cousin Dora, fully cognizant her end approached, wanted to speak one last time to those who were special to her. When in a coma for almost three weeks before her death, the medical personnel could not comprehend what in heaven's name was keeping her alive.

At this point her kidneys were failing, her lungs filled with water, and she had a weak heart. In short, Cousin Dora was hanging on by a thin thread. In fact, her nurse asked her to give herself permission to die. Her daughter, Doris, told me later that at Sunday Mass Doris sensed that Cousin Dora had wanted to say "Goodbye" to someone she loved.

Doris described to us in a letter that she went home and tried to think whom that person her Mom waited for might be. Then, miraculously, that Sunday evening, Richie appeared at Dora's bedside after a long bus trip from Albany, New York. Cousin Dora wanted to see Richie one more time before she died. She died the next day at peace with the world. Doris thanked Richie for granting her Mom's last wish.

I then returned to the Albany area and took a job as an insurance representative for Metropolitan Life Insurance Company. It paid $7,500 a year to start. I needed a car for this job, had no credit, and was thus unable to buy a car. I had no Social Security earnings for the past ten years, the equivalent to an alien who dropped down to Earth from another planet. Fortunately, Nancy's Mom, Mae Hare, co-signed the car loan with me. I then began work as an insurance agent. As an extrovert I would, on occasion, make appointments from the phone book for the entire office of new sales representatives. Not an easy task.

I spent a lot of company time studying for the life insurance exam offered by New York State so I could sell life insurance. After studying for only two weeks, I passed the life insurance exam the first time I tried. I then did the same for the health insurance exam. My boss would try to motivate me by putting pamphlets highlighting new cars in my mailbox. I found this to be amusing rather than a source of motivation. I found the job unbelievably boring. So after six months with Met Life, I quit my job and collected unemployment. As I waited in line every week to collect my unemployment benefits, I felt like a failure.

I then applied for a job involving hypnotism. A "doctor" advertised in *The Schenectady Gazette* that he wanted employees who knew hypnotism to work for him for his company called Hypnotherapy, Inc. I had taken a course in psychiatry while doing graduate work at the University of Wuerzburg. I applied and got the job which paid $350 a week. After taking a two week refresher course in hypnosis, my boss gave me my own office in Poughkeepsie, New York.

I then had to advertise for a secretary and interview potential employees. I hypnotized people to stop smoking and to lose weight. I felt very comfortable using hypnosis. Before the actual session, the client would listen to a tape explaining hypnosis. The actual session with me would only take about twenty minutes and would cost $50 for the initial session.

On some days I would make $300. Some people who came to my office were skeptical whether it would work or not. However, confident in my abilities, I would knock them out. A young man in particular came for hypnosis to stop smoking. After one session he told me that his chronic back pain had completely disappeared. I don't know who got the biggest surprise out of this, him or me. I had no knowledge that he suffered from chronic back pain until after the session.

I only worked as a hypnotist for a few weeks when I learned of a part-time opening in the Department of Philosophy at The College of Saint Rose in Albany, New York. While they were going through my application at Saint Rose, a Professor of Religious Studies quit his position to become Pastor of St. Helen's Church in Schenectady. Father Bertrand Fay at St. Rose then asked me if I would like to apply for the full-time position in Religious Studies. I jumped at the opportunity. There were six other candidates but I got the job, much to my great delight.

I informed my boss, the doctor, about my job offer at St. Rose and he said he was planning in the next few weeks to increase my salary to $400 a week. I told him that I intended on taking the position at The College of Saint Rose. Later I found out that he lied to me. He actually had intended to fire me. I am grateful to Divine Providence that I did not turn down the job at Saint Rose and stay with Hypnotherapy, Inc.

Imagine my shock a few months later when I met the secretary of my boss on the street one day. She informed me that the "doctor" at Hypnotherapy, Inc. was a pathological liar and had no medical credentials. I also read in the local paper that all 21 of his offices were shut down by the I.R.S. (for tax fraud) who confiscated the furniture in all of his offices. Also, instead of sending the F.I.C.A. wages to the Social Security Administration, he had pocketed them himself.

I did remember some of the things I had learned from working as a hypnotist. I taught my twin, Bobby Brown, all that I had learned and he became interested in using hypnosis in his part-time job as psychotherapist. He became a member of a group of professionals, dentists, doctors, and psychologists who met on a regular basis and perfected various induction techniques on themselves so that they could be more helpful to their patients in their various practices.

THE COLLEGE OF SAINT ROSE, 1974–84

I began teaching Religious Studies at The College of Saint Rose in the fall of 1974. I had a tenure-track position in academia and the Department Chair expected me to teach four courses: Christology, Sex, Sanity, and Sanctity, Introduction to Religious Studies and World Religions. It involved an enormous amount of preparation on my part. I loved my students and felt that Saint Rose paid me to do something that I would enjoy doing without remuneration. I recalled the Scot, James M. Barrie's adage, "Nothing is really work unless you'd rather be doing something else."

Two months after I started teaching at Saint Rose, Nancy Hare and I got married. My dispensation from Rome came in by that time and according to canon law I could marry with the blessing of the Church. However, we were not allowed to get married in church which perplexed me. Instead, the ceremony took place in our rented home on Pinewood Avenue in Albany, New York.

The Bishop of Albany, Howard Hubbard, designated Father Bertrand T. Fay as his official witness to our marriage. Father Fay met with Nancy and me separately and jointly before the ceremony to ask us certain questions. One of the questions took me by surprise. Father Fay asked if I were married before, and if so, did I kill my previous spouse? The printed directions on the form indicated that Father Fay's instructions were to ask this question *discretely*.

Nancy planned the entire ceremony. Father Dick Shields drove down from Montreal to perform the wedding Mass. We invited about forty guests. My Dad refused to attend because he was still upset with my decision to leave the Franciscans, but my Mom came, along with my brothers. My twin, Bobby Brown, read one of the scriptural readings and my younger brother, Tom, acted as my best man.

After the meal some folks danced. We sat around in a circle, told funny anecdotes, and had a lot of laughs. I had the jitters before the ceremony and began to have cold feet. I'll never forget how Nancy looked at me during the ceremony when she took her marriage vows. She said the words with so much feeling that I completely melted. I knew then and there that I made the right decision.

That night Nancy and I stayed at the townhouse of her bridesmaid, Edie Toohey. The next day we left for our honeymoon at the Old Inn in Grafton, Vermont. It started to snow on the way and for the last eight miles we rode on an unpaved road running through the forest. Nancy wondered where I was taking her. *Esquire* magazine had an article which rated the Old Inn as one of the top twenty inns in the country. It figured it would be a perfect spot for a honeymoon. The small town of Grafton had a cheese factory, a museum, and an old covered bridge. Nothing beats the charm of New England.

At this time Nancy had taken a position in the Intensive Care Unit (I.C.U.) at Ellis Hospital in Schenectady. After being there for two weeks they put her in charge of the I.C.U. She did that for several months until she got an offer to return to St. Peter's Hospital in Albany to be in charge of two medical floors and a surgical floor of the hospital. After Mark's birth, Nancy still had responsibility for three floors of the hospital, although she only worked part-time.

I thoroughly enjoyed teaching at Saint Rose for the first five years, that is, from 1974–79. When I came up for tenure in 1979 things took a turn for the worse. A colleague did not support me for tenure. He sat on the Tenure and Promotion Committee that unanimously turned me down, voting 5–0 not to give me tenure. A fact he subsequently denied.

Neither did another person on the committee support me. They claimed that I had sufficient publications but that my teaching fell short. Yet the very semester they voted to deny me tenure all five of my courses were closed out with 30 students apiece. Many of my students would sign up for three, four, and five of my courses, although all of them were electives. If I were as terrible a teacher as the committee thought, why would all of these students sign up for them, when courses in Religious Studies were not compulsory?

I found it incredible that my boss, Father Fay, received tenure without even having a M.A., whereas I had my PhD. Both professors who had voted against me had at that time only an M.A. degree, yet they were telling me that I came up short. They had never sat in on my courses or done a formal evaluation so at the time I wondered how they could know firsthand about my teaching.

The story does have a remarkable conclusion. Both the Undergraduate Dean, Don Tappa, and the Graduate Dean, Richard Ognibene, were asked by the President to write a separate report commenting on my abilities as a teacher and as a scholar. Dr. Ognibene and I had written a paper on creative teaching. Actually, Dr. Ognibene asked me to write a first draft of the article, but Dr. Ognibene liked it so much he decided to send it out for possible publication as is. The article appeared in the journal of the College Theology Society called *Horizons*, a refereed journal.

President Manion, acting on the report of the two Deans, granted me tenure and promotion to Associate Professor at Saint Rose in 1984. I could hardly contain myself when I learned that the vote of the Tenure and Promotion Committee had been overturned. Yet this whole matter left a sour taste in my mouth. It made me start looking for another position. In 1984 I interviewed for a position as Head of the Department of Religion at Auburn University. To be honest, I wasn't even sure of the state in which it was located. Close to thirty candidates vied for the position. Based on my PhD. from the University of Munich, I made the final cut and the Search Committee asked me to interview for the position.

I flew down to Auburn in May of 1984 and as part of the interview process had to teach a class. There were 30 students in attendance plus the entire Search Committee: Gordon Bond from History, the Head of the Committee, Bill Davis from Philosophy, Catherine Perricone from Foreign Languages, Jerry Brown from Journalism, and Jim Dawsey from Religion. I had a wonderful interview and absolutely loved the campus.

To my great delight Dean Ed Hobbs called me on Memorial Day, 1984 and offered me the position at Auburn. However, the starting salary of $28,500 for nine months seemed like a low ball figure. However, I knew that Auburn University had a great reputation and that, in time, I would get sufficient raises to make my move to Auburn worthwhile. In the meantime John Kuykendall, Chair of the Department of Religion and Dr. Bond read my scholarly publications and recommended that I be hired at the Full Professor level. That proved to be a boon for me. As I gained seniority at Auburn I would be paid equity money to make up for the disparity between my salary and that of the regional average for full professors of Religion.

The move to Auburn came off without a hitch. We drove down in two cars in tandem. In Maryland we stopped to eat and were seated in the middle of a crowded restaurant. I ordered clams. When they arrived my son, Kenan, said to the waitress, "Are those Ku Klux clams?" We all laughed and told him not to say that too loudly. So he blared out his question in a louder voice, "Are those Ku Klux clams?"

The children were adjusted to the South before the moving van left. Nancy's transition involved much grief. She had a terrible adjustment. After all, she had worked at St. Peter's Hospital for 19 years and felt right at home in the Northeast. She now had to leave family and friends behind and start a new life. She had to leave her $20,000 a year part-time job in Albany and start off making $10 an hour in Auburn.

I, too, had to make adjustments. I missed the excellent restaurants in Albany and the music station that played excellent classical music 24 hours a day. However, I could not believe the warm weather. I did not miss Albany's cold, wintry winters. I soon realized that the South is the most homogeneous region in the U.S. Southerners are also very religious with about 71% belonging to a church. One of the first questions people asked me is: "Have you found a church yet?" Up north no one would ask such a question. It would be considered rude and offensive. I could not believe that people would pry into my personal life. My wife suggested another possibility. Perhaps in asking the question Southerners were interested in having you join their church, their fellowship. After living in the south for many years I realize Nancy had sized up the situation correctly.

The language and cultural differences between the North and the South came as a great surprise. I came to hear such phrases as "ya'll," for "you all," or the phrase "I'm fixin' to," instead of "I'm about to." What really surprised me was to hear folks say, "*Hey* Rich," instead of "*Hi* Rich." I had difficulty understanding some of my students because of their thick accent. In turn, they had trouble understanding me and said I "talked too fast."

After a few years in the South I learned that many Southerners eat black eye peas on New Year's Day for good luck. In a restaurant a man had a button which said, "Keep the South clean; put a Yankee on a bus." The Southerners like to be indirect and non-confrontational. They considered me a typical Yankee because I tended to be too direct, that is, calling a spade a spade. It seemed odd to me when at a college football game before 85,000 fans a student athlete would lead the crowd in a prayer to Jesus. I thought that in a pluralistic society this might be offensive to some religious groups, for example, Jews.

I thoroughly enjoyed teaching and doing research. In my first three years at Auburn I edited a book on *Theology and Authority*, published 9 refereed journal articles, received a major grant for $10,000 from the Alabama Humanities Council, reviewed 10 books in the best journals in my field, and gave eight papers at professional meetings and conferences. Also, enrollments in the Department of Religion were up 27% in the first three years when I served as Head of the Department, as compared with the last four years in which John Kuykendall served as Head.

A very sad incident occurred on September 28, 1988. Dad called from Bayonne and said that Mom had attempted suicide. She had taken about 100 aspirin tablets at once in hopes of ending her life. I almost freaked out. On November 24, 1988 Mom and Dad celebrated their 50th wedding anniversary. I sent them a gift from Americus, Georgia, consisting of pecans, fruit cake, chocolate and coffee from Nicaragua.

On January 6, 1989 I received a phone call out of the blue from my brother, Frank. He said that Mom was missing. This upset me greatly because I knew in my heart that Mom would not be found alive. I had a difficult time coming to terms with this news. The Bayonne Police led by Lt. Colson found Mom's body in Newark Bay between 1 and 2 A.M. completely frozen. They listed the cause of death as suicide and exposure. It snowed hard that day leaving four inches of snow on the ground. It pleased me that Mom's body was found so quickly. If we had waited longer, we would not have found it because of the tide. Maybe Mom had finally found rest. Life had proven very difficult for her. In a sense Mom went through purgatory here on Earth, and now found her peace in heaven.

I wonder now if Mom had entered the initial stages of Alzheimer's disease. Several items lead me to this conclusion. First, she said she had lost the ring my sister-in-law, Theresa, had given her, yet Dad found it in her purse. Second, she wanted Barbara to hug her three times the last week before she died. Third, she forgot to sign the Christmas card she sent us that year. Fourth, her paranoia near the end of her life seemed very pronounced. Perhaps we should have requested an autopsy to see if she had had some type of brain dysfunction.

I asked that the wake last only one day and all parties ceded to my request. I was comforted by the support of my wife, daughter, Nadine, who accompanied Nancy and I to Bayonne for the funeral, by my Dad and four brothers. I was touched by the outpouring of sympathy on the part of my relatives and by the Franciscan presence. Father Juniper preached a beautiful sermon, one that I'll always cherish.

In the days after the funeral I found it difficult to concentrate. I was worried how Dad, Bill, and Tom would handle the loss of Mom. At the cemetery Bob, Frank, and I were the last ones to leave Mom's gravesite prior to her burial. We formed a circle and were energized by holding our arms together and saying Farewell to Mom. We were comforted knowing that she was finally at peace.

Bob and I disagree on the cause of death. I thought Mom had committed suicide, Bob thought otherwise. He thought that Mom had become disoriented on her way home from the store that fateful January day. It was snowing very hard and Bob surmised that Mom accidentally walked into the bay. To some extent the exact details of Mom's death are irrelevant. The tragic fact is she would never be coming home again.

Over the years I have found comfort in these words of Emily Dickinson:

> "I shall know why- when Time is over-
> And I have ceased to wonder why-
> Christ will explain each separate anguish
> In the fair schoolroom of the sky."

BOB'S GROWTH AS A THERAPIST

Watching my granddaughter Leah at play tickles me to death. She lives happily in her own inner world and takes it seriously. She loves to open the cookie jar and say "Hi" to the cookies that are hiding there, even if she cannot have one. In her mind this all makes sense and she enjoys sharing her inner world with me, knowing full well that I take it as seriously as she does. As adults many of us have simply lost our child-like sense of wonder and mystery. Years ago I watched a radio show called "make believe ballroom" time. It is make-believe to those of us who have found another world which we never dare to call "make believe." The world of the child is no more fanciful than our adult world which has lost its sense of wonder and mystery.

When we consider the lives of the early masters of psychoanalysis and psychotherapy such as Sigmund Freud, Alfred Adler, and Carl Jung, we run smack into the same phenomenon. Their lives strike us as unreal, fictional, and make-believe. We assign them such appellations because we cannot grasp the significance or relevance of their lives and ideas in our present, everyday world of make-believe.

I cut my teeth in psychotherapy under the tutorage of Dr. Jeffrey Keefe, a psychologist and Franciscan priest in 1964. He initiated us into the reading of Freud, Adler, and Jung. Trained in the classical psychoanalytic tradition, he transmitted that knowledge to us, concomitant with our study of theology. This same type of training continued for me into the early 1970s at the Christian Institute for Psychotherapy run by Drs. Alphonse and Rudy Calabrese. We used the traditional psychoanalytic couch and sat behind the patient taking notes so that we could be a *tabula rasa* in the Freudian sense and not contaminate the process of the patient.

In the early 1970s I worked for Family Court in Nassau County. There we did not have the luxury of doing long-term therapy in the Freudian tradition. I also felt that the psychoanalytic approach had its definite limitations particularly since the world of 1970s had little in common with the world of these early pioneers of psychotherapy. We needed crisis intervention, substance abuse techniques, and brief family therapy. I studied these therapies at Adelphi University while pursuing my Master's degree in Social Work there. Upon graduation from Adelphi I studied family therapy at Hofstra University and alcoholism at Freeport hospital in Long Island.

When Richie returned from Germany in 1973, he had studied hypnosis at the University of Wuerzburg, Germany under Dr. Wiesenhutter. Richie then worked briefly as a hypnotist in Poughkeepsie, New York. He taught me hypnosis and I continued learning hypnosis at the American Institute for Psychoanalysis and Psychotherapy. Also, beginning in 1975 I met for two years with a study group at Nassau University Medical Center where we practiced clinical hypnosis. One of the members of that study group, Dr. Daniel Araoz, introduced me to Ericksonian hypnosis, named after Milton Erikson, M.D. a famous clinical hypnotist. I purchased the complete works of Milton Erikson and incorporated Ericksonian hypnosis into my practice.

In 1979 I taught family therapy and clinical hypnosis at the Long Island Institute for Mental Health. Shortly afterwards, our group of professionals, a medical doctor, a dentist, a psychologist, and a social worker), started the Long Island Society for Clinical Hypnosis. One of the members of the group, Anthony Gaita, a certified social worker, started giving lectures throughout the country on hypnosis and asked me to assist him. I did this for several months on weekends but I did not enjoy the travel aspect of the job. Instead, Dr. Araoz and I co-authored a program called "Dynamic Imagery", a 16 hour course in hypnosis for laymen and began giving weekly supervisory sessions on hypnosis for professionals.

Dr. Araoz and I were successful in our work with "Dynamic Imagery" and in 1983 we had to make an important decision. We could continue to work 50 to 60 hours a week with Dynamic Imagery or invest some major dollars in a marketing company that would franchise Dynamic Imagery for us. We decided not to go the route of the franchising direction and instead Dr. Araoz continued his writing and teaching and I focused my efforts on my private practice.

In the early 1980s I continued to read the complete works of Milton Erikson as collected by Ernest Rossi. I began to use hypnosis for various addictions such as cigarette smoking, food addiction, and the like, but also for alleviating fears and phobias. I found hypnosis helpful even with very disturbed patients. They could be taught self-hypnosis. This managed to give them a certain control and sense of self-mastery that enabled their self-esteem to increase. I have discovered by reflecting on my own experience as a hypnotist the uncanny healing power of the human mind. I endeavor to pass on this tremendous lesson to my clients. Almost every single school of psychotherapy and hypnosis, particularly Milton Erikson and his followers, upholds this tenet about the vast powers of the human mind.

How precisely do the psychoanalyst and the hypnotherapist differ in their approach to the unconscious mind? Freud and Adler listened to their clients, analyzed their dreams, and gave the client their interpretations somewhat passively. This amounted to an insightful and intellectual way of gleaning meaning from the client's unconscious thinking and dreaming. The hypnotherapist, on the other hand, induces a trance state in clients, actively reworking and redirecting the material of stories, ideas, and images that bubble up from the unconscious. When a client tells me a dream in the waking state, I can, with the client's permission, ask him or her to be hypnotized and dream the same dream as before. Then I supply the client with a different outcome, one therapeutically favorable to the client's self-esteem. This leads to a resolution of the problem.

In June of 1987 I attended a workshop at the Omega Institute in Rhinebeck, New York on Holotropic Breathwork, given by Jacqueline Small who, along with Stanislav Grof developed this technique. It involves deep breathing, hypnosis, loud music, and altered states of consciousness. This new model of the human psyche rejects the dualism of mind versus body, cause and effect, solid space and linear time in favor of a holographic or holonomic model of psychic processing. According to the holonomic principle everything in the psyche mirrors everything else. It no longer matters whether we start in therapy with the trauma of birth, childhood, or the body. Each of these aspects can take the therapist into the feeling core of the psyche when properly pursued.

Whether we start with a thought, a vague memory, a pain, an ill-defined feeling, or even a breathing pattern, we find ourselves moving quickly in and out of several levels of psychic reality into worlds within worlds. In a single two or three hour session a client's inner journey may go from a recent distressing event in a past life, to a memory of birth, to a childhood incident, perhaps even to an archetypal or transpersonal awareness. During this workshop at the Omega Institute I personally experienced my own birthing experience. The following year I traveled to a suburb of Salt Lake City and spent a full eight days attending a seminar given by Jacqueline Small on Holotropic Breathwork in August, 1988.

When in January, 1989, my mother drowned, my heart broke in half. A friend of mine, Msgr. Tom Hartman, told me that he could arrange for me to see a psychic by the name of George Anderson. In April of 1989 I spoke to George and he remarkably told me about my mother's death with uncanny accuracy. He began by noticing a strong feminine presence around me and I indicated that it might be my Mom. The first words she said to him were, "Frank, Frank, don't blame yourself. I fell into the ice and drowned. I tried calling for help but no one could hear me because of the blizzard raging that day. I did not suffer but went quickly once I gave in to the water." Mom went on to describe other relatives and friends who greeted her when she passed over including Anne, but at this point George Anderson said, "She's shaking her head. It's not Anne but Anna," apparently a reference to our paternal grandmother who crossed over two months earlier.

Anderson went on to describe other relatives who greeted my mother on her arrival on the other side. I found the entire experience tremendously consoling. It genuinely helped me in my grieving and healing over her loss. This experience with George Anderson set me on a course to study the realm of spirit. In this connection I studied spiritualism, a philosophy, a theology, and a religion in its own right. Spiritualism began in 1847 when the Fox family in Hydesville, New York moved into a house where a mysterious rapping noise could be heard. Her mother and her two daughters discovered a way to communicate with the rappings by knocking back and discovered a code to talk to the so-called "spirit," who revealed that a man had been murdered in the house. Mrs. Fox and her daughters found that they could speak to the spirits of the dead and so the modern séance was born.

I attended a weekly study group led by spiritualists at the Sanctuary of Infinite Spirit in Smithtown, New York. In my first workshop that I attended in 1997, I saw the spirit guide of the workshop leader walk through the room. She had reddish hair and a hazy, yellowish garment around her body. This fascinated me. Shortly afterwards, my daughter's father-in-law passed away. The group leader told me that there was a life insurance policy next to a hand-carved marble chess set sitting in a dresser drawer, the fourth one from the top. I informed my daughter's mother-in-law who indicated that their insurance papers were kept there. Neither my wife nor I had ever been in her house so this lent authenticity to the revelation.

In 1998 and 1999 I volunteered my time to become a group leader of a workshop on bereavement in my local church. A couple attending the workshop lost their 21 year old son in Florida while jogging with his father. One day I saw the image of the son sitting on a park bench with his grandfather. This park bench had a smooth metal rung on the bottom of it, much like the kind one would find on a rocking chair. Afterwards, I related these events to the young man's parents who told me that the grandfather worked in the metallurgy lab of the New York City Parks Department. As a result of this and similar experiences I became convinced that the deceased do no die. Rather, one can communicate with them and vice versa. It's possible for individuals to increase their vibrations so that spirits can contact them.

HYPNOSIS AND HYPNOTIC REGRESSION

I usually define hypnosis to my clients as "an altered or changed state of awareness, perception, or concentration." As the direct opposite of sleep, hypnosis may be thought of as an intense form of concentration in which the client will not lose consciousness but feel extremely relaxed and comfortable during the session. In my professional practice I have used hypnosis successfully to handle phobias, panic attacks, weitght control, anxiety, depression, impotence, insomnia, jealousy, test anxiety, self-consciousness, and to stop smoking. Hypnosis also works well for both past life regression and present life regression.

Once while using present life regression, a client told m that she had witnessed her father killing her mother. Concerned that she might not be consciously aware of this, I induced amnesia for that memory so that the client would not be traumatized by that event. In subsequent sessions using hypnosis, I worked with her to face this painful reality and deal with her feelings of anger, betrayal, and loss so that she could move on with her life. I remember well another client noting where exactly she was while under hypnosis, since she reported that she could only see blackness. As it turned out the client found herself in 17th century France with a black blindfold on her eyes, awaiting the guillotine. This sounded bizarre to me. However, another client who saw only black found himself upside down in deep, dark water, making it virtually impossible to see anything. He related that he found himself in this dark water after his plane crashed.

Anyone witnessing a session where a client relates experiences from a past life that illuminates present existence naturally asks the question, "Did the client really remember such events or make them up?" This question, in my opinion, can't be answered with a simple "Yes" or "No" answer because it's complex. There exist three plausible interpretations to this phenomenon of past life regression. First, the memory may well up from a person's unconscious memory. Second, it may be a memory derived from the collective unconscious of humanity, viz., the archetypes that Carl Jung has written about extensively. Or, third, it may be a communication from an entity or spirit that has crossed over to the other side. That entity or spirit may desire to open up a new line of communication with us individually.

During the past fifteen years that I have conducted sessions of past Life Regressions, I've found that it does not matter how the communication is achieved. Rather, more importantly, the communication helps a client better cope with a defeat in life, a fear, a trauma, or an open psychic wound. To be honest, I have personally used past life regression myself during the past several years. In doing so I have been in touch with my many past lives. The first one occurred in the 13th century when I saw myself as an early follower of St. Francis after that saint died. I sported a tonsure and wore an early Franciscan habit or tunic.

The second occurred in 16th century Germany in the area known as the Black Forest, that is, the area around Freiburg-in-Bresgau. I had married and had fathered two small children. My wife had abandoned me for someone else. This fear of abandonment carried over with me into my next lifetime in

18th century America. I pictured myself as a wounded Confederate soldier riding in the back of a horse-drawn cart en route to a medical facility that would look after my war-time wounds. A feeling of resignation and defeat came over me as well as a strong sense of powerlessness. I realize this may sound hard to believe, but this has indeed been my experience.

In reflecting over my present life I notice some of these same psychological elements, namely, a fear of abandonment, an attraction to the Franciscan lifestyle, and a sense of powerlessness. The fear of abandonment harkens back to the year 1947 when my mother had a nervous breakdown, then faced confinement to a mental hospital for the next twenty years. My brother, Richie, and I were attracted to the Franciscan way of life because of its emphasis on poverty and community life. We could say of the Franciscans what the early Christians in the *Acts of the Apostles* said to each other, "See how they love one another." The feelings of powerlessness derived from our childhood when we had no input into where we would live or with whom.

DREAMS: THE ROYAL ROAD TO THE UNCONSCIOUS

We dream a half dozen times a night and upon awakening in the morning we often have a recapitulation dream that summarizes the past night's dreams. Usually we'll forget our dreams unless we write them down immediately upon waking. A passage in the *Talmud* states: "A dream that has not been understood is like a letter that has not been opened." In psychotherapy I encourage my clients to mention their dreams. To facilitate the remembrance of them I ask my clients to keep a pen and pencil handy near their nightstand and to write down their dreams as soon as they awake in the morning.

I use this format in analyzing my patients' dreams:

1. Narration of the dream taking particular note when the dream occurred
2. Associations connected with the dream
3. The feeling tone of the dream, e.g., happy, sad, angry, joyful
4. Since the raw material of the dream flows out of one's experience that day, I ask the client to go through the events of the day
5. I ask the client how they interpret the dream
6. Based on my knowledge of the person, the client's associations and feeling tone, and what the client has told me about the dream, I offer my interpretation of the dream

ON ACTIVE IMAGINATION

What is the active imagination? It differs from dreaming insofar as one is awake and conscious during the process. Active imagination might best be understood as a dialogue with the various layers of one's self as found in the unconscious mind. Instead of dreaming, one enters into one's imagination while fully awake, allowing images to float up from one's unconscious mind. Then, one talks to, and interacts with, these images from down below. These images, in turn, answer back, expressing different points of view from those of one's conscious self. In short, while dreams happen at the level of the unconscious, in active imagination images occur on the level of the imagination. These images occur neither on the conscious nor on the unconscious levels. Rather, they occur at a place that combines the conscious and unconscious levels.

The essential element of the active imagination is one's conscious participation in the imaginative experience. The ego actually saunters into the inner world, walks and talk, argues and confronts, making friends or enemies with those it finds there. One's ego actively takes part in the dreams in one's imagination, engages other actors in conversation, exchanges other points of view, and participates in shared adventures. When done correctly, the active imagination pulls together the various parts of one's self that are in conflict and awakens the person to the different voices inside, thus effecting a peaceful truce between the warring ego and the unconscious mind.

SOUL RETRIEVAL

We have medical doctors who treat physical and mental illnesses while shamans treat spiritual diseases. A shaman may be understood as an ancient specialist in techniques of ecstasy. A famous writer on the history of religions, the late Mircea Eliade describes a shaman as a person who makes a journey in an altered state of consciousness in order to treat illnesses of the soul, interacts with the world of spirit, and on occasion, helps souls cross over to the other world. In short, a shaman treats the loss of soul, a spiritual illness that causes physical and emotional diseases.

Aristotle speaks of the soul as the vital essence or substantial form of the body. What could cause a person to lose his or her vital essence? Generally speaking, a trauma or loss of some kind, be it incest, abuse, surgery, an accident, illness, or the death of a loved one. In many of these traumatic losses one's soul or vital essence separates from us in order to survive the experience by escaping the full impact of the pain. Soul loss can be precipitated by whatever a person finds traumatic, even if another person suffering the same loss might not experience it as traumatically as that person.

When part of the soul splits off and enters another sphere, the person finds him or herself in a debilitated state. In order to recover the missing parts of the soul, the shaman enters into a non-ordinary state or upper world, using drumming in order to retrieve the lost soul of the client. The shaman then brings the lost soul of the person back to the ordinary, empirical world. When I work as a shaman in my office, I usually use drumming to get myself into a non-ordinary state of mind. I always invite a third person to be present during the ceremony. We usually begin by praying to God to help us in our journey and I consciously attend to the lost soul of my client. At the outset I am unaware as to what region of the other world I will be drawn. At times, I have violent shakes or suddenly, find heat leaving my body or have other physical reactions.

The eagle remains my power animal that helps me on my spiritual journey. Normally, I hold a crystal in my hand and give my client a crystal to hold. Once I locate the person on the other side who is holding back the essence of my client's soul, I usually give that person a golf ball that glows in order to facilitate the release of the hold they have on the client's soul. At the conclusion of the ceremony I blow the essence or fragments of the lost soul into the crown and heart chakra of my client. Then we sit in silence for ten to fifteen minutes. Afterwards we discuss together where I had gone, what I experienced, and who it was that held the client back. We then pray together and thank God for creating wholeness again in the client.

Let me now describe a case history using the fictional name of a client. John X came to therapy because of an excessive attachment to Marissa, a woman who was not his wife. His emotional attraction and attachment to Marissa did not make sense on the practical level. Yet no matter how much he knew intellectually that this relationship had the potential to destroy his marriage, he could not end the relationship with Marissa. Even after Marissa died suddenly and unexpectedly, John still felt a primitive connection to her and on one level wanted to end his marriage, even though he knew that he loved his wife and she loved him.

After much discussion and soul-searching, we performed a "soul retrieval" in order to help Marissa let go of her hold on John, so that he could proceed with his life and with his marriage. I asked John to bring a close friend to the session with him. We lit candles, spread out an Indian blanket on the floor, and prayed together for a successful outcome to our endeavor.

We began by listening to a recording of music from drums. Drumming can take a person to an altered state of consciousness. We lay down on the floor, side by side, and I eventually entered a state of altered consciousness. All the heat left my body and I began shaking. Finally, led by my spirit-guide (Bruce) and by my power animal (an eagle), I entered the lower regions where I stumbled on Marissa in a very dark place. In order to allow her to release her hold on John, I gave her a gift of a glowing golf ball. Then I began my ascent to the material world of everyday life. When I awoke, I blew the wind over the head and heart of John, symbolizing the release of his grip on Marissa.

After the ceremony we thanked the spirit-guides for their help. We then asked John to spend an hour in the woods meditating and thanking the spirit-guides for their help in making him a free man. Believe it or not, this ritual had, indeed, the desired effect. John gave up his attachment to Marissa and carried on with his life.

COUNTING OUR BLESSINGS

1. We felt the hand of God gently guiding us after we left the Franciscans. Richie felt fortunate in finding a tenure-track position at the College of Saint Rose, while Bob lucked out in securing a position as a probation officer in Nassau County, Long Island.
2. If Richie had never taken a course on hypnosis at the University of Wuerzburg, the odds are that neither he nor Bob would have worked as hypnotists. It's amazing how many small turns in the road can be a major factor in the unfolding of one's life. What we often perceive as chance may not be chance at all, but part of a Grand Design.
3. Both twins have discovered that one's life can be very rewarding by helping others find themselves. The secret of happiness is forgetting oneself and caring for others. In losing ourselves, we find ourselves. Such is the paradox of life.

Epilogue

"We don't see things as they are; we see them as we are."

Anais Nin

"All the knowledge I possess anyone can acquire,
But my heart is all my own."

Goethe

Bobby and Richie have not lived together under the same roof for about forty-five years. Yet mentally and emotionally the bond between them remains fixed and firm. How do we account for this? All of us have within ourselves a handful of individuals who hold a special place in our inner world. These folks constitute a "community of the heart." Our most powerful feelings relate to them. We always live in the presence of these special individuals who are both outside and inside us. They are so woven into the fabric of our being that we seem never able to come to terms with them, no matter how long we live. These key individuals walk into our lives in a myriad of ways. They are usually family. These special individuals loom large in our memories, our psyche, and even in our dreams. One of us kept a dream diary and noticed that our twin always seemed to pop up in practically every dream.

Although we have lived about for most of our lives, we seem to have some kind of mental telepathy. When Richie studied in Austria, he developed stomach problems and often had a headache probably caused by living in a high altitude. Interesting enough, Bobby developed the same symptoms and knew that Richie was sick although Richie did not tell anyone in the States about this so that they would not worry. We often have a sense that the other twin will call us on a particular day. We also have the same likes and dislikes in

113

terms of food, cars, and people. Both of us eat peanut butter every day for breakfast almost as a ritual. We both love flashlights and have bought dozens of them over the years. We even prefer the same type and model of car. Unbeknown to the other we each bought a Toyota Camry a decade ago.

As of this writing God has given us 68 years of life on planet Earth. Our bodies seem to have aged physically. For instance, we tend to lose our balance easily, particularly on a roof or ladder. Our feet hurt us a great deal toward the end of the day. Our reflexes have slowed down. No longer would we be kingpins playing table tennis the way we did as teenagers. We now wear bifocals and cannot easily read the numbers in the phone book without wearing thick glasses.

Yet, somehow, we do not feel old mentally or psychically. Our inner spirits remain young and vibrant, although time, that omnipresent tyrant, seems to have speeded up as we have aged. Our birthday seems to come along every month not every year. We are both mentally sharp although creaks and cracks appear at times in our short time memory. There exists a huge chasm between how our bodies feel and how our inner spirits see things. Aristotle of old had it right. We, humans, have a mortal, physical body but an immortal, spiritual soul. The soul appears to us to be timeless, ageless, and ever new. Our bodies, on the other hand, are subject to the law of entropy.

The thought of death and our own mortality frequently crosses our minds. Maybe that's a tipoff to the fact that we're in the evening of our lives. As youngsters death appeared distant to us. Death always happened to someone else. We could be tranquil and objective about it. As senior citizens the thought of death follows us like a shadow. We are constantly reminded to think of the one thing necessary- to love and serve the Lord and all humanity. We now read the obituary columns and notice that many people who have died were younger than we are. That's a scary thought.

Bob and his wife, Theresa, have two children, Kristin and Mary Beth. Kristin received her B.A. in East Asian Studies from Harvard and works for Oracle, while Mary Beth got her undergraduate degree in social work from Syracuse and her M.S.W. from New York University. Rich and Nancy have a son Mark, an attorney, who graduated from the University of Alabama School of Law with his J.D. degree, Kenan, who received his M.D. from the University of Alabama, Birmingham, and then did his residency in psychiatry at the University of North Carolina, Chapel Hill, and Nadine who graduated from Auburn University with two undergraduate degrees and is now pursuing her M.S.W. degree at the University of Alabama, Tuscaloosa.

We find ourselves wanting to leave something of our spirit to our children and grandchildren. That's the main reason we wrote this memoir, that is, so future generations would know what it was like to live in the twentieth and twenty-first centuries. We do not know how many days we have left and we particularly want our grandchildren to remember us as persons. What better way for them to know us than through this first-person account? Granted that our children could conceivably tell their children about their grandparents, however, this way they can read it for themselves and make their own judgments. This memoir pays tribute to the human spirit of two boys from Bayonne, New Jersey, who wanted, in some infinitely small way, to share their story and become immortal. As the German adage asserts, *Wer schreibt, bleibt*, or "Those who write, live on."

We have led satisfying and fruitful lives. We have taught our children how to fish, how to swim, and how to drive. In fishing the main thing swims below the surface and it's not the fish we have in mind. One goes fishing not necessarily to catch fish but to bond with one's children. To fish is to engage in a common, transcendental task that takes us out of our ordinary everyday world. Fishing gives us alone time with our children, to discuss what really matters in life in a leisurely fashion.

We have attempted to give our children good example knowing that values are caught rather than taught. We have tried to be generous with the poor and downtrodden and hope that our children and grandchildren will have noticed this lesson. One cannot tell a child not to smoke if they see us lighting up a cigar or cigarette after an evening meal. Actions always speak louder than words. Children seem to have antennas that take in all that we say and do. And these antennas are highly impressionable, taking in our hidden attitudes. Most of our communication with our children, and even with our grandchildren, takes place unconsciously and subliminally. Not only do we pass on genetic qualities to our children, but we also given them our entire value system. They even mimic our mannerisms. When Richie's son, Mark, for example, was one years old, he carried himself exactly like his Dad.

One of the hardest things we have faced in later life is this: our children have to learn some of life's lessons on their own. We cannot tell them how to live. They have to find out for themselves through a sometimes tortuous process of trial and error. As parents we have to look on helplessly as they learn from their mistakes, particularly in regard to relationships. We have had to bite our tongue while sitting on the sidelines, rather than telling our children what to do in a particular situation. This has, at times, been a struggle, causing us much pain and anguish. It involves letting go, a chief component of the grief process.

We hope and pray that our children will have imbibed some of our spiritual values such as prayer before meals, the importance of spending time with the Lord on a daily basis, and trusting in Divine Providence. Those who are religious have a deep sense that God speaks to them by means of the events of daily life. Those who are pious tend to have an upbeat, optimistic view of the future in the teeth of global warming, economic uncertainty, and the spread of the H1 N1 or swine flu virus.

In life on Earth there's no such animal as perfect security. If the President of the United States can be assassinated as in the case of John F. Kennedy, (who had a protective circle of Secret Service personnel around him), then no one can be perfectly secure. We live out our lives in fear and trembling. The sage or wise person must often hang on by a thread. This appears to be dangerous but not if one remembers that God holds the other end of the thread. The wise person takes what comes in life and deals with it deftly, that is, making the most of every situation. To trust in the Lord means to take what life throws at us and to come up grinning.

In a sense every symphony goes unfinished. And that's true of every life. We all have ambitious plans for the future. Some will pan out, others won't. When on sabbatical for the 2009–2010 academic years I (Richie) wrote a long list of things to do. For example, I wanted to update my knowledge of Spanish and Arabic. I never accomplished that. However, I did read widely in many areas and finished this memoir which has been on the backburner for eight years. That's par for the course that is life. I also did enjoy good health this past year, relaxing from the stress and strain of teaching every day. In a sense what we do in life matters little in the grand scheme of things. God does not need our work, though we have to do our work of remembering Her, despite the many distractions we face daily.